Dear Terri,

Keep shining your light, the world needs beautiful souls like you.

Thank you for being there on my journey

Jeanette

x.



Thank you to....

The Big Lottery Community Fund
Art By Ella Bell
Poetry by Vicky Ryan
Book Design by Done For You Divas

Lyndsay, Lundy, Susan, Amanda, Lizzie, Sarah, Lisa
Whitney & Ash
Kathrine, Sue, Hannah, Crystal, Leigh
Ali, Sarah, Tina, Julia & Michelle
Leonie Dawson
The Purple Arrows, Tuesdays Coffee Club
Wendy & Helen
Lundy Bancroft & Bill Babbage

Without out you this book would not be here.

THANK YOU

COMMUNITY FUND

" PERHAPS THE BUTTERFLY IS PROOF THAT YOU CAN GO THROUGH A GREAT DEAL OF DARKNESS, YET STILL BECOME SOMETHING SO BEAUTIFUL "

# Welcome To Our Workbook

## Introducing the Directors & Facilitators Jeanette Brown and Debbie Coleiro

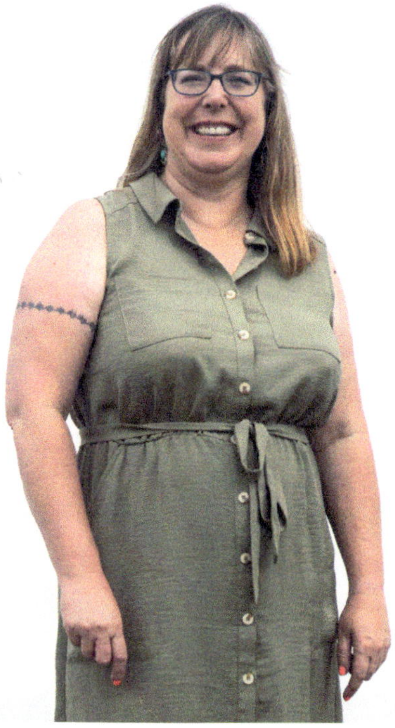

Hi,
We are Jeanette Brown and Debbie Coleiro and we are excited to bring you the Empowerment After Domestic Abuse workbook and eCourse.

We have both delivered Pattern Changing for many years and realised the importance and value of the course in aiding the recovery of those who have survived domestic abuse.

Both of us are professionals in the field of Domestic abuse and have lived experience we have used this knowledge and experience to create our own course and workbook with the feedback and input from our course participants as to what works best for them.

We are delighted to present to you our work book and course and really hope it helps you take steps towards a more positive future.

Best wishes Jeanette & Debbie

## Introducing the Artist-Ella Bell.

I am a Devon-based artist and have been tattooing professionally since 2015. My work is mainly inspired by nature, symbolism, magic, mythology, and the body. I love my job as a tattooist, and I also really enjoy print-making, painting and illustration, as well as photography and ceramics. I love it all! I believe creating, in all of its forms, should be available to everyone, and can be a great source of self-expression, freedom and healing.

# Forward

I attended a course called Pattern Changing in 2010. Not only did it give me the life skills to move forward with my life but something quite drastic happened on the last day which lead me on the path to where I am now.
There was a government change and funding to the domestic abuse services was drastically cut. It was announced that the course I had just finished would no longer be running.
Something had to be done about keeping such amazing courses running. I volunteered for the organisation, SAFE (Stop Abuse For Everyone). I worked my way up into different roles and sporadically we delivered courses, dependent on small pots of funding here and there. Everyone I worked with was inspirational and have all played a part in my journey.
I moved to Splitz (Devon Domestic Abuse Support Service) as a DASA (Domestic Abuse Support Adviser) and in 2015 started this little CIC with the main aim of getting this course to others.
Add life experience, everything I learned from my colleagues, campaigners and mentors and you find our course, with deep routes in that course I attended but brought right up to date and available to all, not just the women who experienced abuse.
At last with the new Domestic Abuse Bill we feel things are happening. Abuse and its impact are beginning to be recognised. I really hope that people find the strength to reach out and accept support.
This book has been a dream of mine for so long, it's taken a while to get there. Thank you to everyone who attended our courses in 2020 and for your valuable feedback to make this book happen. I also want to thank my colleague Debbie for stepping up to the challenge and sharing this journey of More Positive Me with me. Your patience and level headedness were just what was needed for our wonderful little CIC.

Jeanette

# Previous Course Attendees

## And What They Have To Say

We have amazing course attendees who have helped us put this book together. We have worked closely and listened to them, taking their suggestions on board and made changes. Many people who have attended our course have joined our peer support groups and share their experience to inform our work. Throughout the book you will see their quotes and input to the book. We are entirely grateful to them and it has been an honour to watch them flourish and grow.

Here is what they want you to know about starting the course...

"Just take the first steps, because however hard it feels. This course will help you in some way, it will change your life."

"I could not recommend this course more highly!"

"The course has given me a positive toolkit and insight that I can start to take steps to move on with my life. Everyone should do the course whether they have been in an abusive relationship or not.""

"There is no doubt in my mind that it helped every single participant focus on what they wanted moving forward."

"I do believe that this course is a life saver in more ways than one! It's an absolute life-changer."

"I can understand your feelings, but if you can just get yourself through that 1st session, it will change your life for the better! "

# Before You Start

## Complete the pre-course exercises.

It's really important that you are out of the relationship before completing this workbook and the eCourse. We named it Empowerment After Domestics Abuse for a reason. If you are in an abusive relationship, or you are not sure if your relationship is abusive, then contact your local domestic abuse service. You can also look at the web pages for Refuge, Women's Aid & Mankind, or call the 24 hour helpline 0808 2000 247. Your safety must come before anything else. Perpetrators do not want you empowered, they will see it as a threat.

Don't skip any part. The book is layered so every part lays a foundation for the next part. Use the eCourse to aid you. There are Q&A calls at the end of each chapter, if your questions aren't answered there then email any questions to info@morepositive me.co.uk or join the peaklivingnetwork.org for safe and secure peer support email plndevon@morepositiveme.co.uk. You are not alone, you are just lead to believe that you are.

"This book will be useful to anyone who has been in an abusive relationship or suffered domestic abuse. Anyone who would like to rebuild their confidence, self-esteem and learn how past relationships have effected your life, emotions and choices. Finally that it is possible to rebuild and discover yourself again." Course attendee/book reviewer.

# Pre-Course

## Before We Start

THERE ARE 365 days IN A YEAR

24 hours IN A DAY

THAT'S 1,440 minutes

TRY AND MAKE AT LEAST 10 OF THOSE minutes FOR you.

# PRE-COURSE

Being ready to learn and focusing on you and your wellbeing.

- Where Are You on Your Journey?
- Setting Course Expectations
- Your Bill of Rights
- Self-Care - Journaling

## The Main Aims of this Chapter:

- To make sure you are in the roght place to start the course.
- To provide a starting point for your journey..
- To give you the opportunity for peer support through the peaklivingnetwork.org

# Where are you on your journey?

Colour in the one that feels the most like where you are now and pop the date on the sheet. We all reach different stages at different times. We will use this to reflect on at the end of the course. There is no right answer - maybe you could write a little about how you are feeling right now, particularly as you are just starting out on this voyage of discovery.

# Setting Expectations

Set intentions to complete the course & set a goal

1 - I will work through the book every...

2 - Or I will work for...(insert amount of time)

3 - I will...

. ...to take care of me.

4 - If I am struggling I will...

5 - By the end of the course I will...

# Bill of Rights

I have the right to be me.
I have the right to put myself first.
I have the right to be safe.
I have the right to love and be loved.
I have the right to be treated with respect.
I have the right to be human - not perfect.
I have the right to be angry and protest if I am treated unfairly or abusively by anyone.
I have the right to my own privacy.
I have the right to my own opinions, to express them and be taken seriously.
I have the right to control my own money.
I have the right to ask questions about anything that affects my life.
I have the right to make decisions that affect me.
I have the right to grow and change (and that includes changing my mind).
I have the right to say NO.
I have the right to make mistakes.
I have the right to not to be liked by everyone.
I have the right to control my own life and change it if I am not happy with it as it is.

# Bill of Rights

"I still have my bill of rights which I have stuck to my fridge door. Again this was very overwhelming to learn I always had these rights and how many have been taken away from me during my lifetime."

"I always look at my bill of rights on the fridge. It has allowed me to speak my mind in my new relationship and I feel more comfortable as a person."

"The bill of rights, the 1st time seeing that was amazing, there was so many of my rights that just weren't being implemented or were being walked over by people, it was a real eye opener! Even now I need to keep reminding myself of my bill of rights and that it is OK to say NO."

# Your Bill of Rights

Read through the Bill of Rights, take your time.. Everyone has these rights. Do you feel that you have all of them? Or are some difficult for you? Write the ones here, in the clouds, that you don't feel you have right now.

Colour in your Bill of Rights, print one out & put it up somewhere you will see it daily.

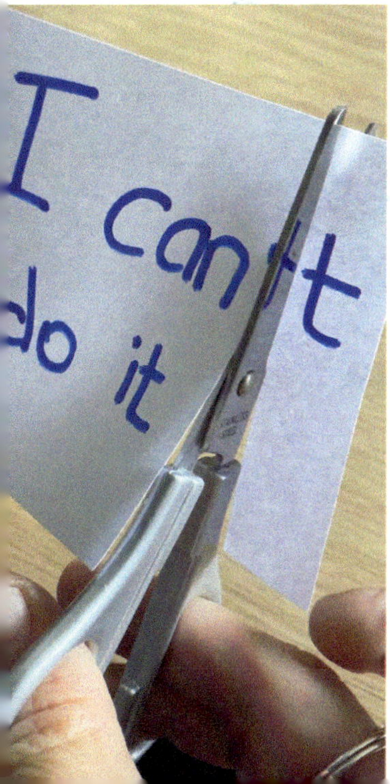

# Journal Writing

Writing can do wonders for your wellbeing.
Have a go at journaling. This can be in different ways for different people so you need to find what suits you the best. When our minds are overwhelmed and things go around and around, it's good to write them down. The very process of writing offloads and takes ideas out of your head and puts them onto paper.

Maybe doodling or drawing will help you when you don't know what to write. You can even cut out pictures of things you love and that inspire you - it doesn't have to be neat and tidy and it doesn't even have to make sense. It can be a place where you start to discover yourself and make sense of what's going on for you.

Do a little smiley or sad face in the corner if you are going to visit it daily. When you start to get in touch with your feelings again, write how it feels, where you feel it and be curious about the emotional and physical effects it has on you. Write it down and let it go.

# CHECKLIST - PRECOURSE

**You've done it, well done! Complete the checklist before you complete your 7 days of journaling and move on to the next chapter.**

- [ ] I have oloured in the figure who was most like me on my recovery journey right now and put the days date on the page.
- [ ] I set my course expectations and set a target for the end of the course.
- [ ] I coloured in my Bill Of Rights and put a copy up somewhere I can see it every day.
- [ ] I started a journal so I can write down what comes up for me as a way of processing the information. This can be a notebook or specific journal, I have or will choose something I like.
- [ ] I connected with others on my healing journey on The Peak Living Network #hub-devon-uk - email info@morepositiveme.co.uk with your request to join our group, or discover it for yourself at peaklivingnetwork.org

# CONTENT

# Chapter 1

## What Is Abuse?

# CHAPTER 1 WHAT IS ABUSE?

We discover what abuse is and its different dynamics and cycles.
It's important to complete this in your own time and process the information.

- A few words from those who came before you.
- The Government Definition of Domestic Abuse
- What is Domestic Abuse?
- The Power and Control Wheel
- The Cycle of Abuse
- Self-Care and Gifting
- Self Care Ideas

THERE ARE **365 days** IN A YEAR
**24 hours** IN A DAY
THAT'S **1,440 minutes**
TRY AND MAKE AT LEAST **10** OF THOSE **minutes** FOR **you**.

## The Main Aims of this Chapter:

- To understand domestic abuse and its different dynamics.
- To offer hope as you take your first steps towards controlling your own life.
- To establish self-care as part of your weekly or even daily routine.

# A Few Words from Those Who Came Before You

"You're so brave for putting up with everything you have, but you are worth so much more and you're stronger than you know."

"Believe in yourself, everything they tell you and the way they treat you is their internal problem. Find your own path, what you love and positive times will follow. You are worthy, you are loved, keep being you."

"The only way to get a different result is to do something different. Of course it takes courage and for some the risks may be so great as to bring fear of dreadful reprisals. There are people who can help you. Experts in their field who have often experienced the same as you. Seize the moment, access their help and the rest will be history."

# The Government Definition Of Domestic Abuse

"Any incident or pattern of incidents of controlling, coercive or threatening behaviour, violence or abuse between those aged 16 or over who are or have been intimate partners or family members, regardless of gender or sexuality" This can encompass, but is not limited to the following types of abuse:

psychological • physical • sexual • financial • emotional

"Controlling behaviour is: a range of acts designed to make a person subordinate and/or dependent by isolating them from sources of support, exploiting their resources and capacities for personal gain, depriving them of the means needed for independence, resistance and escape and regulating their everyday behaviour. Coercive behaviour is: an act or a pattern of acts of assault, threats, humiliation and intimidation or other abuse that is used to harm, punish, or frighten their victim."

The Government definition, which is not a legal definition, includes so called 'honour' based violence, female genital mutilation (FGM) and forced marriage, and is clear that victims are not confined to one gender or ethnic group. It has been widely understood for some time that coercive control is a core part of domestic violence. As such the extension does not represent a fundamental change in the definition. However it does highlight the importance of recognising coercive control as a complex pattern of overlapping and repeated abuse perpetrated within a context of power and control.

https://assets.publishing.service.gov.uk/government/uploads/system/uploads/attachment_data/file/142701/guide-on-definition-of-dv.pdf

Looking at the definition of abuse and different types of abuse, write down in each zone what that looks like. For example, financial could be not allowing you to work or further your education, keeping control of the finances, giving you an allowance or asking for you to account for every penny, spending money that was meant for bills, not paying child maintenance etc.

Financial

Physical

Sexual

Emotional/Psychological

What is the one word that explains all of these behaviours?
Write it in bold across the whole page.

# Power and Control Wheel

"Abuse, who knew it could take s
many different forms? Things tha
just thought were because of me
started to be explained. Things
weren't actually all my fault like I h
thought for years!"

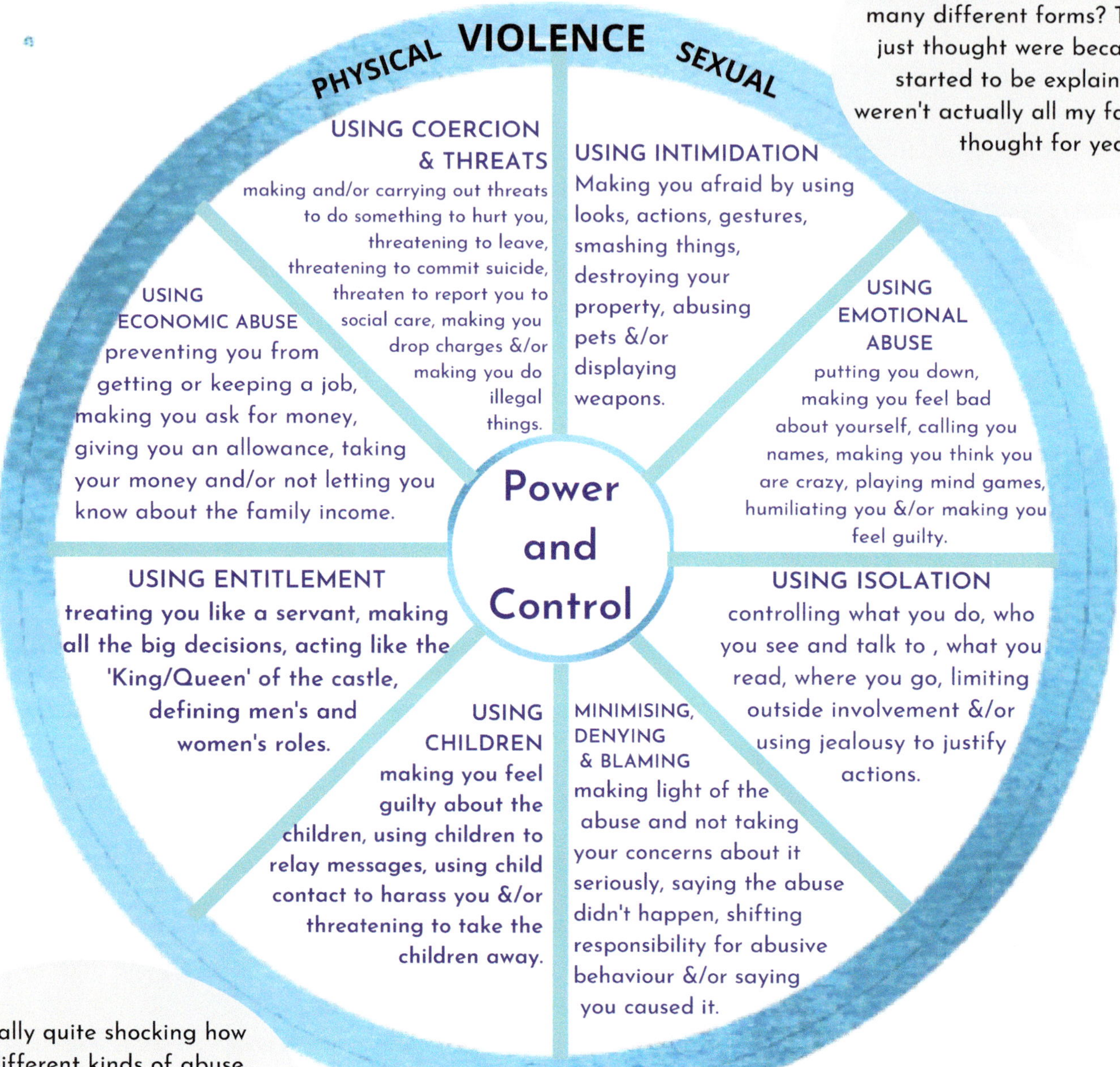


"It's really quite shocking how may different kinds of abuse I had been through. This Power and Control Wheel was a big part of the acceptance of what I had experienced."

The Power and Control Wheel taken from the Duluth Wheel shows the different types of abuse and how they show themselves. Highlight the ones relevant to you. Usually when those forms of control stop working, then violence occurs. Power and control over you is the dominating theme.

" IT IS NOT THE BRUISES ON THE BODY THAT HURT. IT IS THE WOUNDS OF THE HEART AND THE SCARS ON THE MIND." AISHA MIRZAREAD

# Cycle of Abuse

**Insert the words into the right part of the cycle. 'Honeymoon' can be anything from buying flowers to just no abuse or a period of calm.**

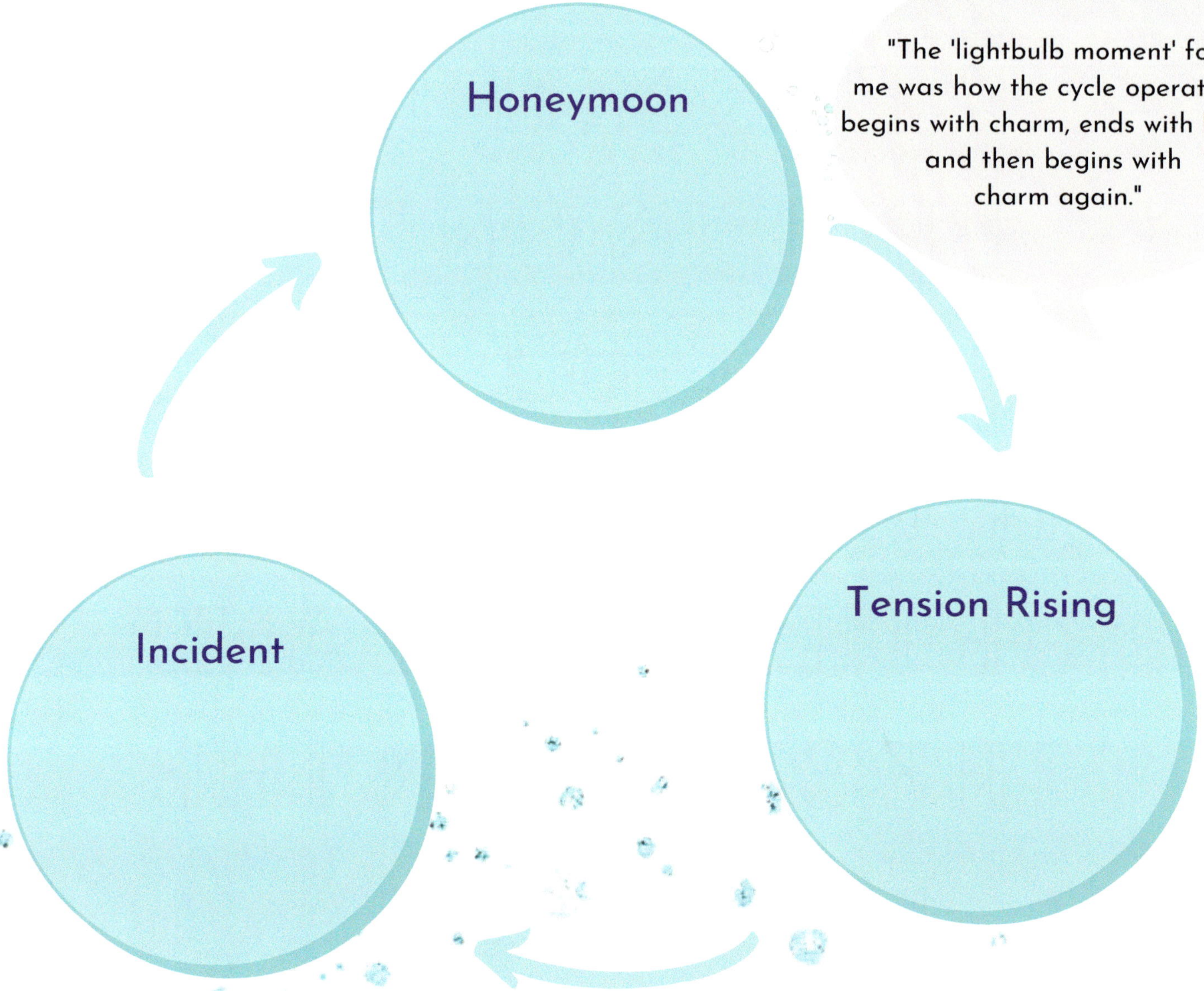


"The 'lightbulb moment' for me was how the cycle operates. It begins with charm, ends with harm and then begins with charm again."

Window of opportunity to leave. Where would you put it in the cycle?

Describe each phase and how they feel. Here's some words you can use:

Walking on eggshells - Shouting - Violence - Argument
Buying you flowers - Sulking - Slamming doors - Glare
Silent treatment - Saying sorry - Threats - Asking for another chance - Acting as if nothing has happened

# Self-Care and Gifting

Well done for getting through chapter one. We suggest you now take a week of reflection before you start the next chapter. These next pages will help you with that.

We talk a lot through our course about self-care and gifting. It really is the secret ingredient to success on this course.

Consistency is vital to your success on this journey. Set a good time each day to look at your journaling pages - a page or even a paragraph or a sentence at a time will do. This in itself is committing to your self-care. It is a gift you are giving yourself; it is honouring yourself. Have the mindset that this is your time and create a new pattern of doing this for you.

"THERE IS NO FAILURE, ONLY FEEDBACK. WHEN WE LEARN FROM OUR FEEDBACK WE GROW."
ROBERT ALLEN

" BUILDING YOUR RESILIENCE WONT FIX THE CHALLENGES WE ARE FACING, BUT IT WILL DEFINITLEY MAKE IT EASIER TO COPE WITH THEM! "

SALLY GUNNELL OBE

# Self-Care Ideas

ꞁERE ARE 365 days IN A YEAꞁ
24 hours IN A DAY
THAT'S 1,440 minutes
TRY AND MAKE AT LEAST 10 OF THOSE minutes FOR you

Here's some inspiration. It's really important to do this for you and an essential part of this course.

Write your own ideas then give them a go.

| | | |
|---|---|---|
| Go for a walk | Take a bath | Take 10 minutes to close your eyes and focus on your breathing |
| | | Colouring In |
| Indulge in a hobby | Have a really good belly laugh | |
| | | Drink water regularly |

# CHECKLIST - 1

**You've done it, well done! Complete the checklist before you complete your 7 days of journaling and move on to the next chapter.**

- [ ] I completed the exercise on the Domestic Abuse Definition and added one word that explains all the behaviours - CONTROL..
- [ ] I completed the exercise on the Power & Contriol Wheel and highlighted or underlined the ones relevant to me..
- [ ] I completed the exercise 'Cycle Of Abuse'. Described each part of the cycle and put the window of opportunity just after the 'incident'.
- [ ] I completed the exercise about self care and filled in the gaps with some ideas of my own.
- [ ] I will now complete seven days of journaling to process the information I have learned in Chapter one.

# Chapter 2

## Why Is It So Hard To Leave?

# CHAPTER 2
# WHY IS IT SO HARD TO LEAVE?

One of the most asked questions is "why don't you just leave?" We explore the family dynamics through domestic abuse and the barriers to leaving.

- Who Is Responsible For The Abuse?
- The Excuses I Made.
- Challenging Your Thinking.
- Why is it so Hard to Leave?
- Addictions.
- Georgian Window.
- Self-Care. - Who Am I?

## The main aims of this chapter:

- To examine the issue of who is responsible for the abuse
- To explore the concept of love as an addiction.
- To understand why it is so hard to leave an abusive relationship

" IT IS NOT THE BRUISES ON THE BODY THAT HURT. IT IS THE WOUNDS OF THE HEART AND THE SCARS ON THE MIND." AISHA MIRZAREAD

# Who Is Responsible For The Abuse?

Abuse is ALWAYS the fault of the abuser. Victims tend to blame themselves for something they have or have not done. They develop coping strategies to give themselves some sense of control over the situation, including blaming their own actions or trying to find ways to 'manage the abuse.'

Complete the exercise below with the things that are within your control and the things that are out of your control.

**out of my control**

Other peoples actions, reactions and responses/ Anything outside of my being

**within my control**

myself, my actions, my words, my reactions and my responses

# You are not Responsible for the Abuse.

As a victim of abuse, consider if you have any control over the abuse.

You will find that you will be blaming yourself. Write your excuses for the abuse that make you feel as though you have some control over it. For example:
'If I had done this.... then it wouldn't have happened'
'If I hadn't gone out......'
'If I had gotten dinner cooked on time.....'
'If I had been a bit more organised.......'
Add your own.

They usually start with 'If only I had done this.....'. Or 'I acted this way and that's what started them off.....'. Or, you excuse the behaviour for their mental health, stress at work, drinking problem and so on.

Leave a space between each one so you can come back and write a little about it when you are ready.

# The Excuses I Made

# Challenge Your Thinking Around Who is Responsible for the Abuse.

- The abuser's problem comes from their deep-seated need to control and display power.
- The victim is powerless to control or change the abuse.
- You did not cause it and cannot control or cure it.
- You are not responsible for it.
- Being a repeat victim is learned behaviour and can be unlearned.
- Abuse is solely the responsibility and problem of the abuser.
- The abuser never has the right to hit their partner, demean them or abuse them in any fashion.

# Why is it So Hard to Leave?

"I didn't leave because I didn't have anywhere to go. I was financially dependent upon my partner. I was threatened with harm if I left and my children were also threatened with harm."

If you are on our course, it is because you are now out of the relationship or you have distanced yourself from your abuser. Reflect on how you have come to this point. You didn't just say 'OK, I'm out, goodbye'. It may have taken you months, if not years, to mak the decision to leave. So, what were your barriers to leaving? Here are some of our previous course attendees' answers. Colour in the ones that are the same as yours and add your own.

I still loved him/her

The kids needed their dad/mum

They said they would kill me if I left

I was told I had made my bed, so I must lie in it

I had nowhere to go

I didn't want to be a single parent

I kept hoping they would change

They said they would kill themselves if I left

I didn't want my marriage to fail

I couldn't afford to leave

"I didn't want my son to have come from a broken home. I guess I wanted the fairy tale. I always blamed myself for why my ex/abuser behaved the way he did and did the things he did. I believed if I changed, it would make things better."

# Addictions

What can we be addicted to? Fill in as many things as you can. Give them all a positive and a negative attribute. For example, a positive of drinking wine is to 'relax and unwind' but a negative could be 'a hangover' or 'relying on it as a coping mechanism'.

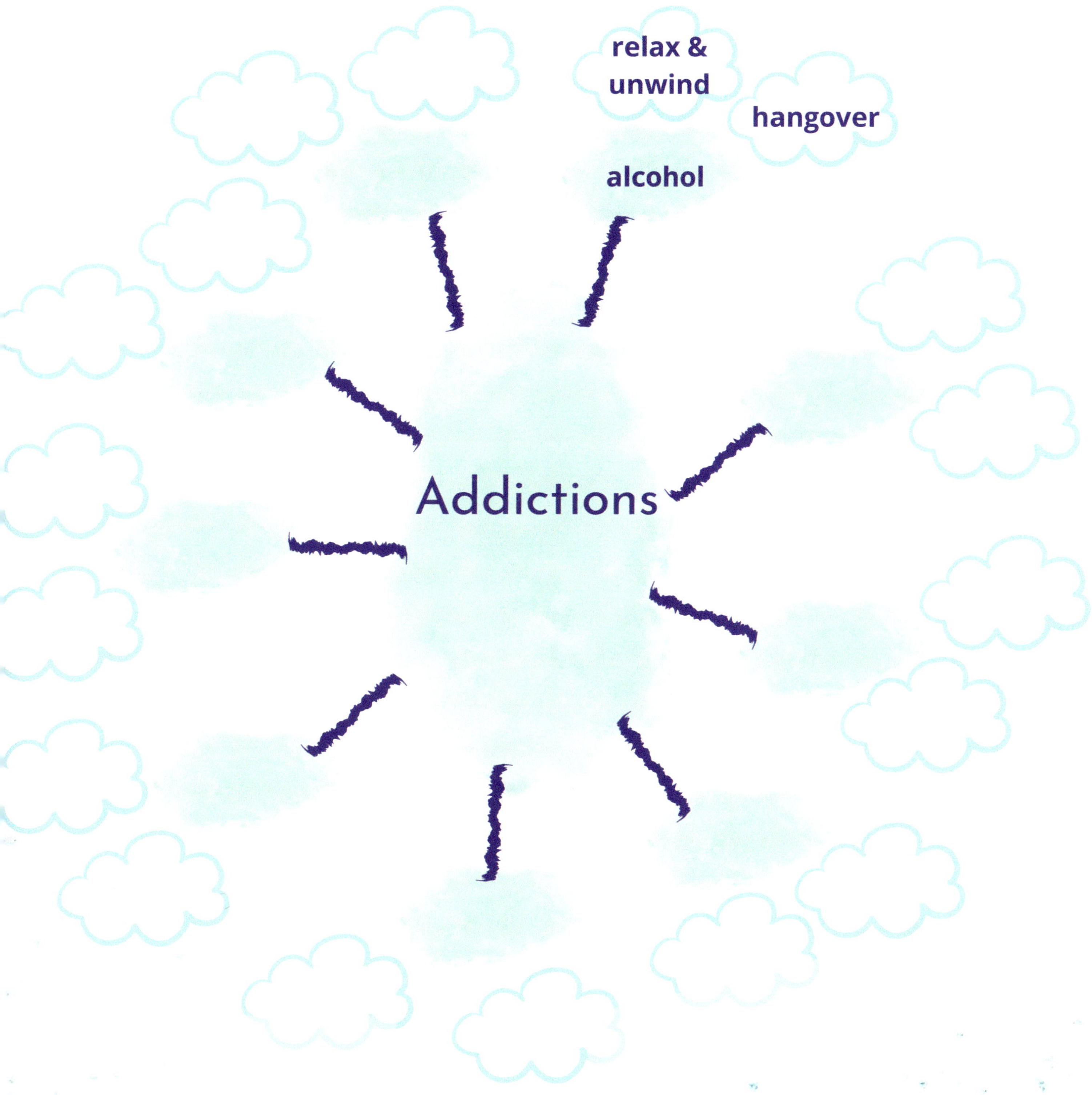

# Addicted to Love or a Relationship

Do you consider love or a relationship as an addiction?

'One may define addiction as a compulsive physiological or psychological need to surrender oneself to a substance, behaviour, or person, even when he or she is aware that it is harmful and self-destructive. Some manifestations of addiction are compulsivity, loss of control over one's own behaviour, inability to leave the situation despite damage and danger to one's self and ones children and denial of the existence and severity of the problem. The presence of any or all of these factors makes leaving the abuser particularly difficult.'
Marylin Shear Goodman & Beth Creager Fallon - Pattern Changing For Abused Women.

Distancing yourself from an abusive person is hard and it can leave a huge vacuum in your life. Like any other addiction.

Let's take a look at the Georgian Window.

video

# Georgian Window

Imagine for a moment that life is like a Georgian window. An abuser will take up most, if not all of the window panes. You may also have work, children etc.

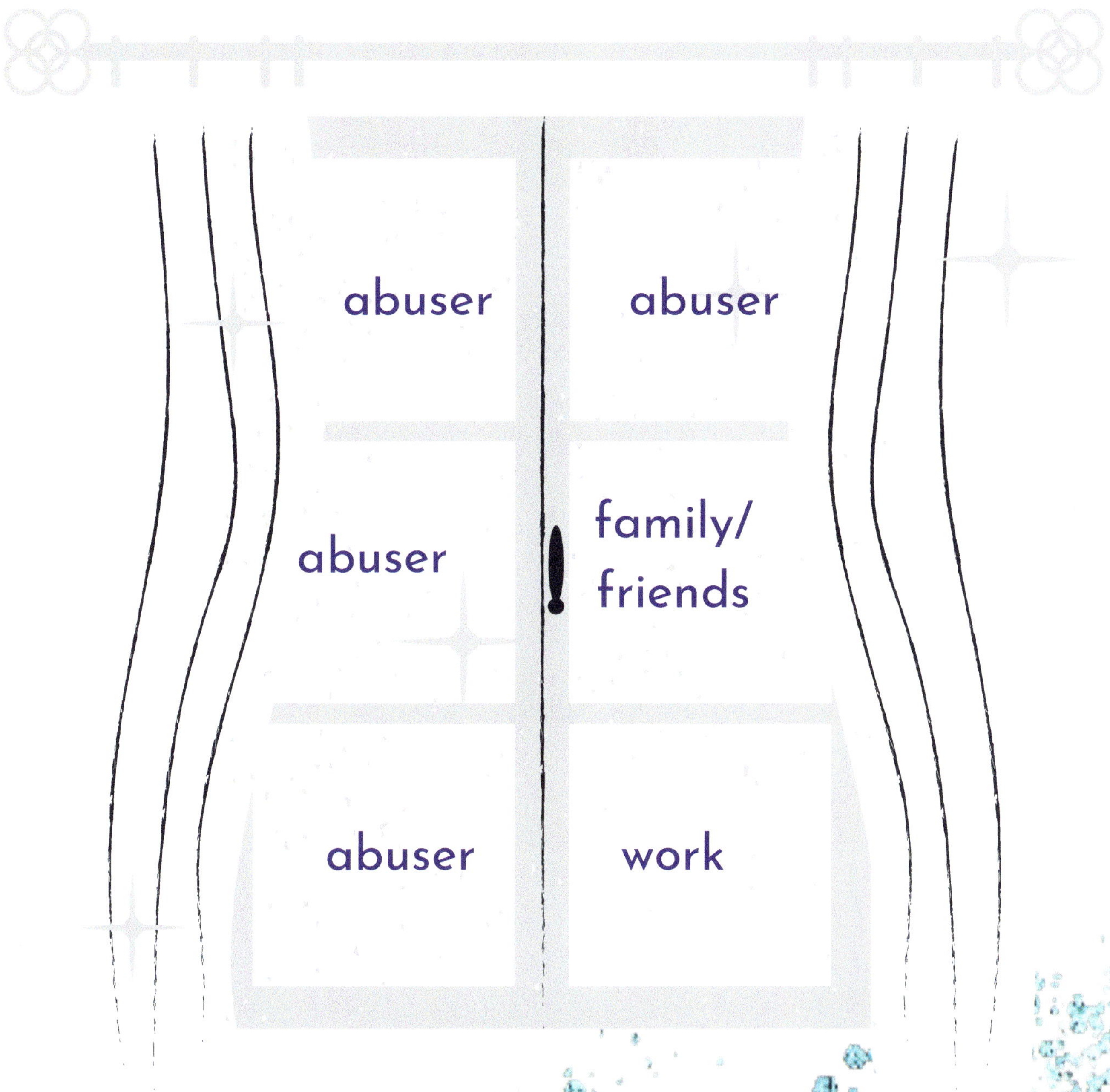

When you take out the abuser, there is a void left.

When something leaves the Georgian Window, we very quickly fill that void as we are so used to living at that high level of functioning and anything lower than that will feel quite boring and that we are 'flat-lining'. For example, giving up smoking can often be replaced with comfort eating. We love the highs, but unfortunately with the highs come the lows.

The voids are often quickly filled, usually with unhealthy replacements.
You can begin to deal with your addictions by recognising and acknowledging your addiction before starting to develop and practice new habits, one day at a time.

What will you fill your window with?

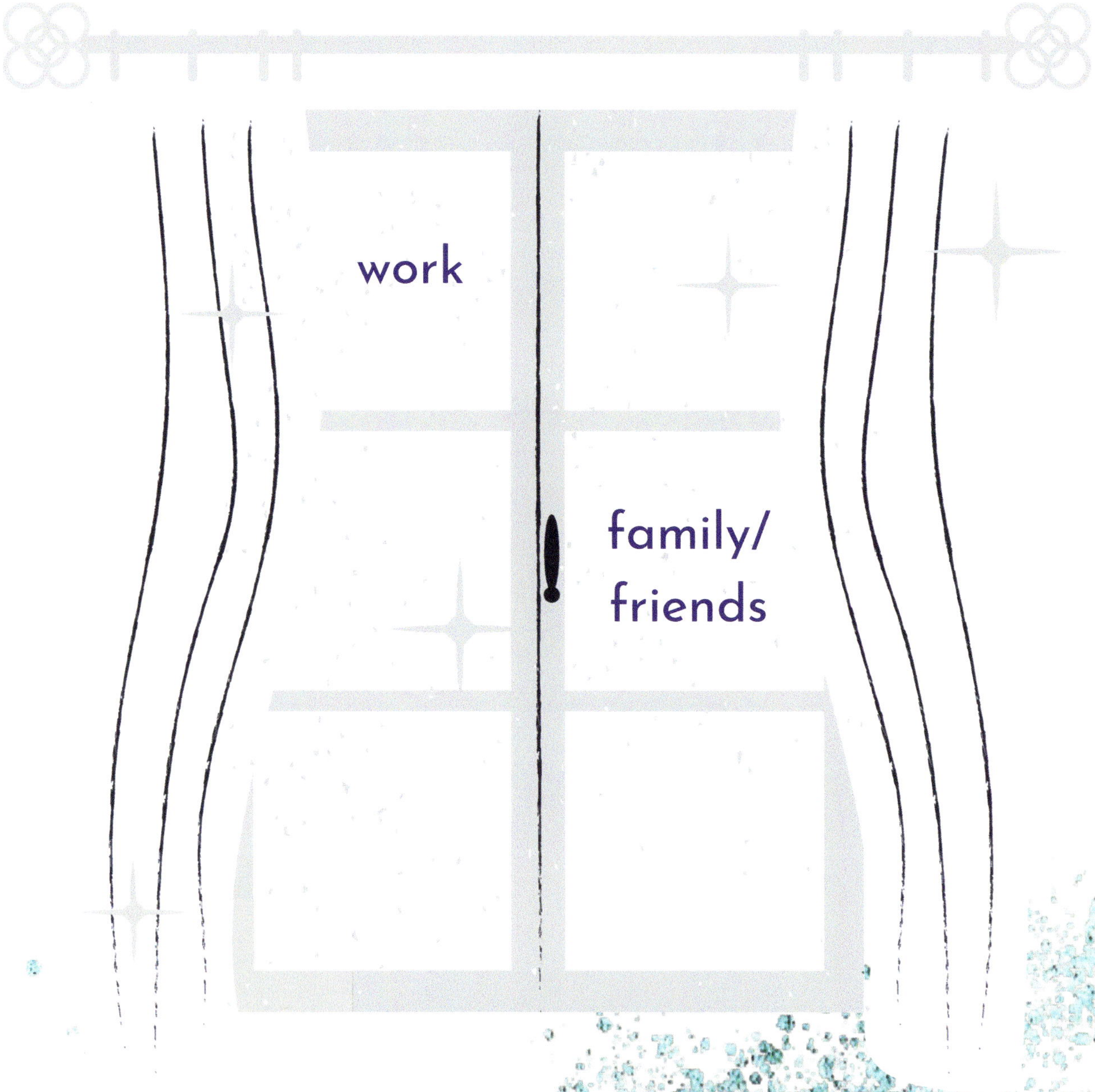

# SELF-CARE WHO AM I?

Draw a picture of yourself in the middle and around it, answer the questions.

The answers may come easily but if they don't, be curious! Give it a go. If you start down the path of negatives, then stop. Only positives are allowed here. This may need exploring over a few days. Add to it when ideas come to mind, either on the sheet or in a journal. It needs to be something you revisit, especially on the low days.

What is your favourite colour?

What brings you joy?

What do you enjoy?

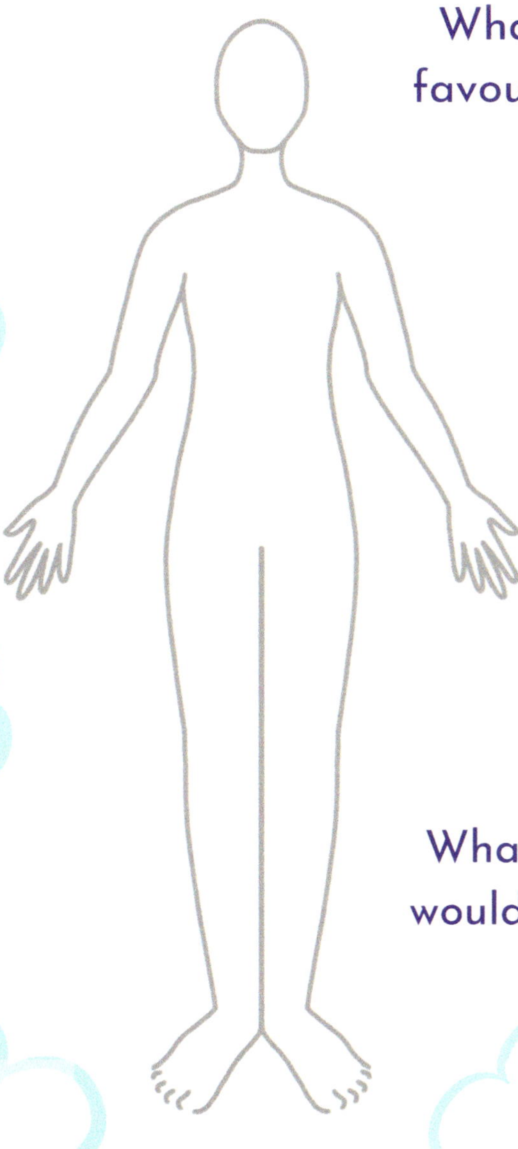

What is your favourite food?

What is your favourite music?

What places you would like to visit?

# CHECKLIST

Check in and see if you've completed each task at the end of Chapter 2. Well done, these first 3 chapters are the most challenging to work through, keep going, you are doing amazingly well!

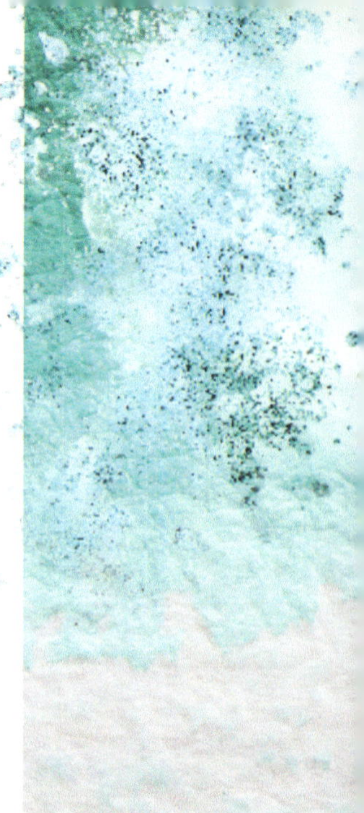

- [ ] I have read through who is responsible for the abuse and understood I am not responsible for the abuse.
- [ ] I completed the 'excuses I made', worksheet and left space for me to come back to as I learn more.
- [ ] I coloured in the reasons I found it hard to leave that matched the ones on the sheet. Added some of my own.
- [ ] I completed the spider diagram of things we could be addicted to, along with the positives and negatives of each.
- [ ] I added to the Georgian Window to fill the void.
- [ ] I completed the self-care worksheet 'Who Am I?' and drew a picture of myself.
- [ ] I will now complete 7 days of journaling before starting the next chapter.

# Chapter 3

## Childhood Legacy

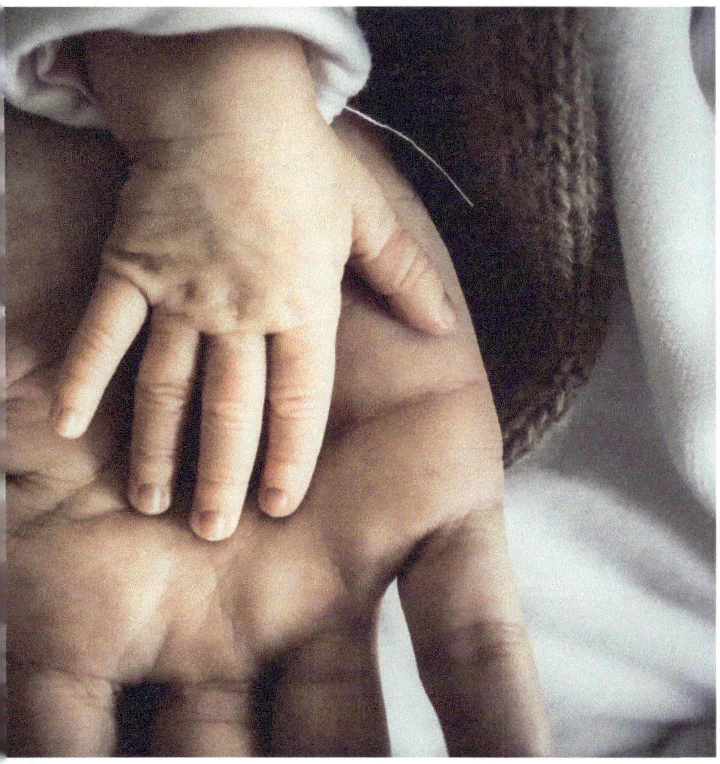

# CHAPTER 3
# CHILDHOOD LEGACY

We explore your own childhood and the family legacy that has left you with. We look at our own childhoods to better understand ourself rather than focusing on ourselves as parents in this chapter.

- Influences Through Childhood.
- Notes & Observations About My Family.
- All Or Nothing Functioning.
- Healthy Family Traits.
- Unhealthy Family Traits.
- The Chrysalis (a poem by Vicky Ryan).
- Self-Care. - Positive Affirmtions.

## The main aims of this chapter:

- To examine the legacy of your own childhood.
- To learn from the lessons our childhood taught us and break unhealthy patterns.
- To encourage you to nurture and value yourself.

# Influences Through Childhood

## What influenced you through childhood?

Start with immediate influences such as parents or family then think beyond to social and cultural.

Notes and observations about my childhood....

Why does your childhood matter?

"Childhood matters because it shapes who we are. How we are brought up affects our life choices, relationships and values".

What can you do to self-nurture your inner child?

"My childhood experiences, my parents' lifestyle and choices have had a negative impact on my life. This still has a direct impact on me now, due to the trauma I went through. Although I already knew all of these things, it was only on the course that I learned how it had impacted my life choices and behaviors. It made me feel very sad and angry. That said, I also felt a sense of relief through sharing with others on the course who had similar experiences as we really never stood a chance because we were all searching for what "we knew to be normal".

## All or Nothing Functioning

Life isn't black or white, yes or no. These are the extremes at either end of a scale of other options. Here's an example:
Self-care is not selfish. Selfish is the opposite end of selfless. Self-care sits somewhere in the middle.

Here are some other examples:

**Black & White** – there are lots of grey shades in between.

**Passive & Aggressive** – there is a whole other way of communicating - we'll learn about assertive later.
**Yes & No** – a whole other spectrum in between.

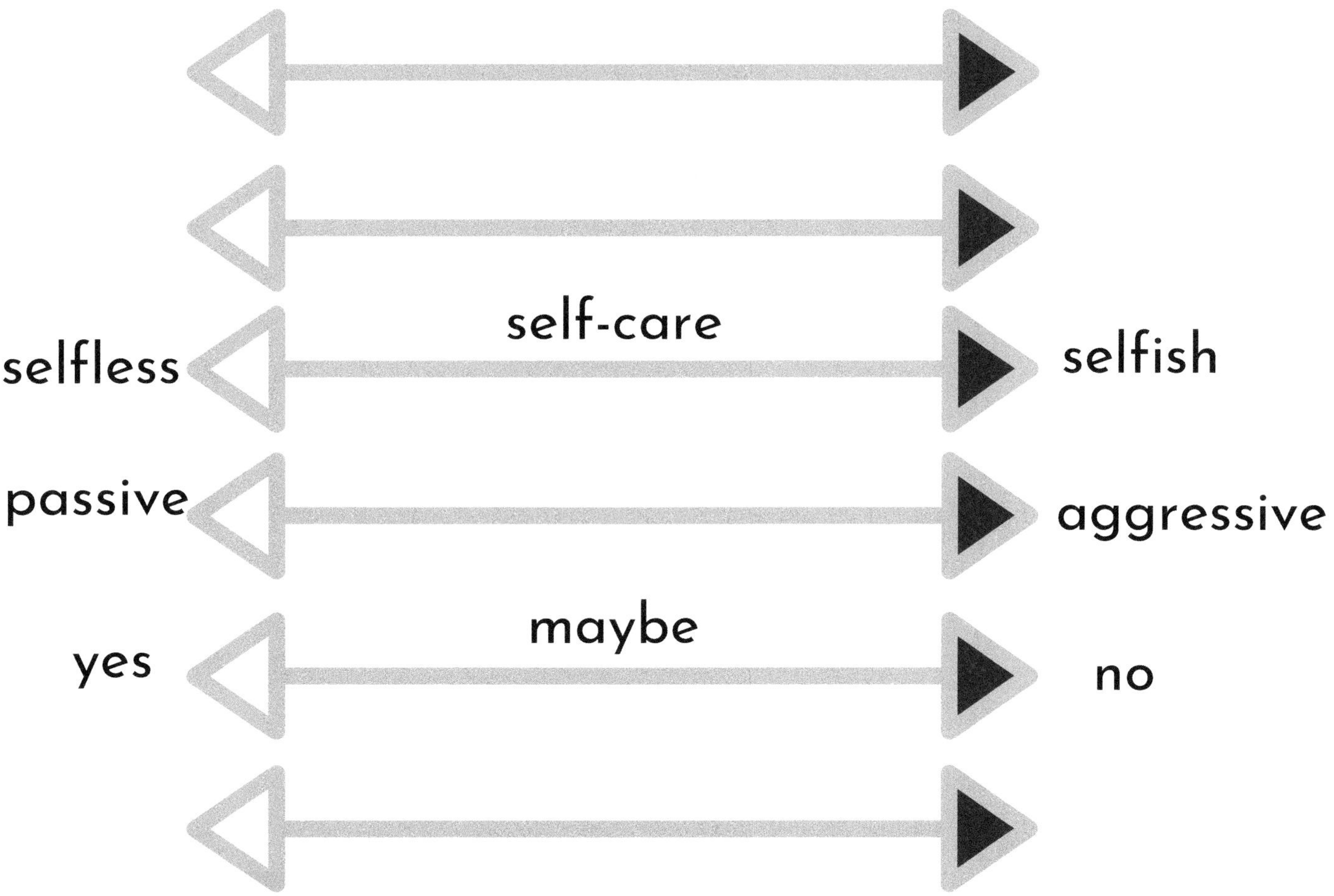

# Healthy Family Traits

What does a healthy family look like?
Think of behaviours, words used, routines and boundaries. Fill in the stars below.

# Unhealthy Family Traits

What does an unhealthy family look like?
Think of behaviours, words used, routines and boundaries. Fill in the circles below.

# The Chrysalis

by Vicky Ryan

Life is like a butterfly, so true for some it seems,
a childhood loved and protected till the day they spread their wings,
but what if that wonderful day never came?
The years kept on passing and things stayed the same,
parents to partners the people did change,
but cocooned by control your whole life is arranged,
for you no decisions, no questions, no ask,
things just mapped out for you, to please is your task,
constantly striving to do your best,
constantly failing every test,
waiting to hear "I love you" "I'm proud",
to open those wings and burst through that black cloud,
it hangs so heavy upon your brow,
but that day never comes, cause you just don't know how?
Surprisingly or so it may seem,
you can reach that day and you can spread your wings,
help, true support and understanding the tools to use,
your dreams are possible with Empowerment After Domestic Abuse..

# Positive Affirmations

Whether you believe a positive affirmation or not, what we repeatedly tell ourselves, we start to believe. Affirmations are about you and start with 'I am', or 'I can...', etc. Today, find some affirmations that resonate with you and put them somewhere you will regularly see them. This could be in your purse, on the front of your journal or tucked into the corner of your mirror. Say them out loud and say them regularly to yourself. The 'Bill of Rights' is a fabulous affirmation. Have you put it on your fridge door yet or somewhere else where you will see it daily? Find our page on Facebook so your daily feed starts to fill with affirmations that resonate. Download the affirmations below or create your own. Put them where you will see them - on your desk at work or pop one in your kids lunch box. Write your favourites in your journal. They will give you hope and build self-belief.

I am a beacon of love and compassion.

Each day of my life is filled with joy and love..

I am good enough.

I wake up happy and excited every single day.

My life is filled with love and compassion.

I find opportunities to be kind and caring...

# CHECKLIST

**You've done it, well done! Complete the checklist before you complete your 7 days of journaling and move on to the next chapter.**

- [ ] I completed the Influences through Childhood exercise.
- [ ] I made notes about my childhood.
- [ ] I found two examples of All or Nothing Functioning and added them to the page.
- [ ] I found 8 Healthy Family Traits and added them to the exercise.
- [ ] I found 7 Unhealthy Family Traits and added them to the exercise.
- [ ] I cut out or created my own positive affirmations.
- [ ] I will now complete 7 days of journaling before moving on to the next chapter.

# Chapter 4

## Grief, Fear & Guilt

# CHAPTER 4
# GRIEF, FEAR & GUILT

We explore and reconnect with our emotions Grief, Fear & Guilt and discuss why it's so important to feel these emotions and understand them.

- Grief.
  Grief Definition.
  Cycle of Grief.

- Fear.
  The Science.
  5 F's & When They Are Useful.
  Decision Making Affected By Fear.

- Guilt.
  What Is Guilt?
  Guilt Check List.
  Guilt Trip Check List.
  Guilt Action List.

  Feeling Your Feelings.
  Thoughts - Feelings - Actions.
- Self-Care - Colouring.

## The Main Aims of this Chapter:

- To connect with our emotions.
- To understand our emotions, their importance and recognise the impact.

"FEELINGS ARE JUST VISITORS, LET THEM COME AND GO."

## Grief Definition

1. Intense sorrow caused by loss of a loved one (especially by death)
2. Something that causes great unhappiness.

www.audioenglish.org/dictionary/grief.htm

Here are some more words to describe grief.

sorrow
agony

misery
torment

pining
blues

woe
heartbreak

sadness
affliction

anguish
suffering

lament
remorse

dejection
despair

pain
heartache

distress
mourning

bereavement

angst ·
mortification

# Cycle of Grief

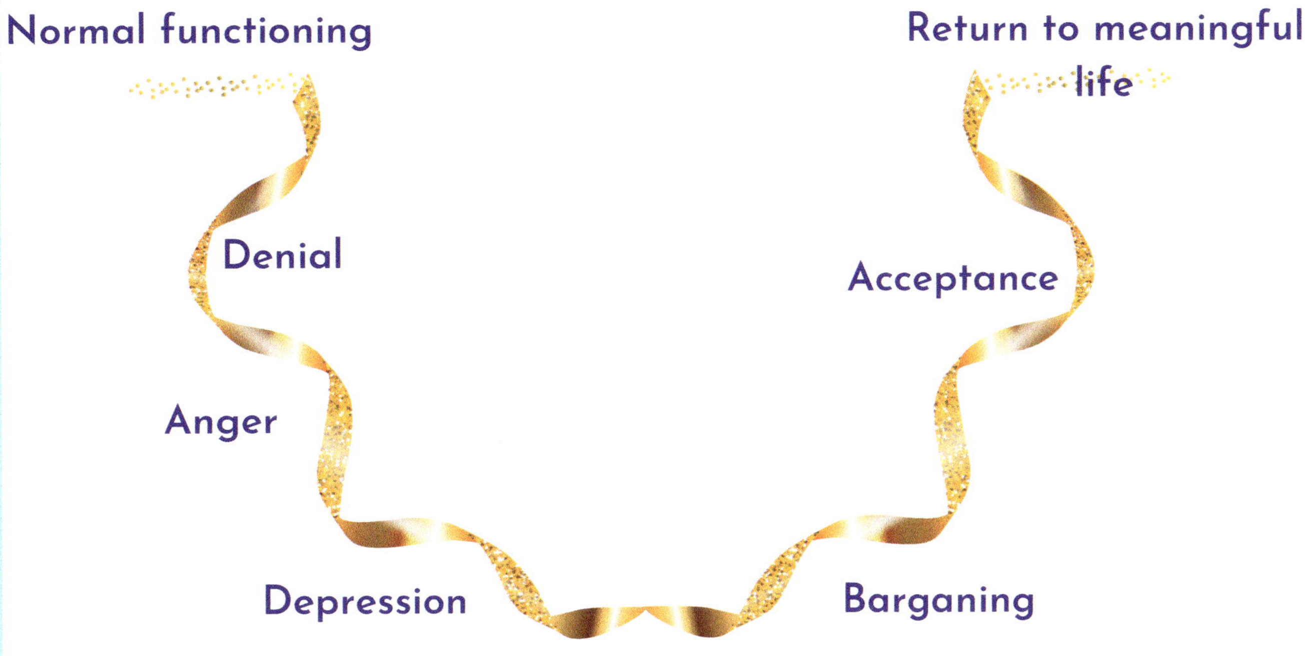


https://www.mind.org.uk/information-support/guides-to-support-and-services/bereavement/experiences-of-grief/

It can feel all consuming, and like the Georgian Window, leave a hole in your life. We can grieve the loss of a relationship, even if it wasn't good. We grieve the loss of hope that things would work out.

# The Cycle of Grief

## Denial

Feelings of shock, disbelief, panic or confusion are common here. "How could this happen?", "It can't be true".

## Anger

Blaming yourself, blaming others and hostility are all common feelings and behaviours - "Why me?", "This isn't fair", "I don't deserve this".

## Depression

Feeling tired, hopeless, helpless, like you have lost perspective, isolated or needing to be around others. "Everything is a struggle", "What's the point?".

## Bargaining

Feelings of guilt often accompany questions like "If only I had done more", "If I had only been...".

## Acceptance

Acceptance does not mean that somebody likes the situation or that it is right or fair, but rather it involves acknowledging the implications of the loss and the new circumstances, and being prepared to move forward in a new direction.

# FEAR

The science: Our amygdala, the oldest part of our brain (reptilian brain) was designed for survival. It is a vital part. Our natural instinct, even from caveman days was to stay alive. When this part of the brain functions however, the frontal cortex shuts down as its not required for survival. The amygdala works 70% faster than the conscious brain, meaning you cannot decide how you will react to fear, it's already done it before you've had time to even think about how to react. This causes the adrenal glands to pump adrenalin through the body, as well as cortisol and supplies the vital organs with blood and oxygen and your muscles full of energy. This is only supposed to be for minutes/hours.

Afterwards your body is fatigued, and you rest. When living in an abusive relationship, you live in survival mode. These things that were designed to keep you safe from lions and bears are not meant to course through your body for months and years. It's no wonder you are exhausted. Hyper vigilance can last for years. Common health concerns are Fibromyalgia and ME after long term fear.

The frontal cortex, the learning part of the brain cannot fully function and learning is difficult. Only when you start to feel 'safe' are you ready to take learning on board. Being safe or getting safe MUST take priority.

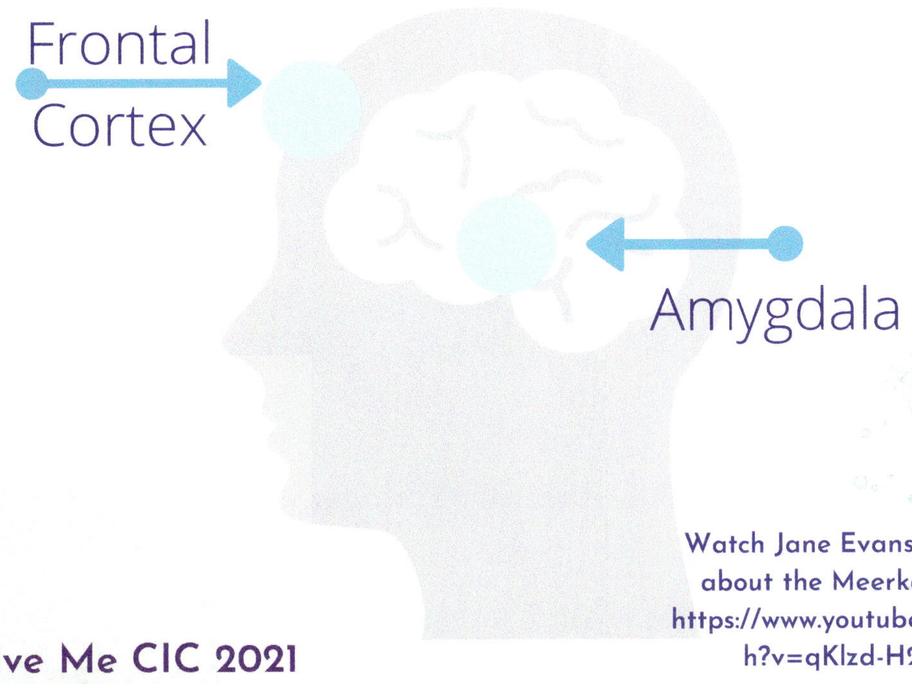


Watch Jane Evans Ted Talk about the Meerkat brain. https://www.youtube.com/watch?v=qKlzd-H2X9w

# The 5 F's

and when they are useful.

## F_ _ _ _

Taking on your opponent because your amygdala has decided that's your best chance of survival. We see this with 'accidental hero's who are then asked 'what were you thinking taking on an armed robber'

## F_ _ _ _ _

The instinct to just get out of there and realise you can run at lightening speed, just to get away.

## F_ _ _ _ _

If there is a Tyrannosaurus Rex keep still it won't see you? Keep really still, no sudden moves.

## F_ _ _ _ _

Used often by children to stay safe , a bully's sidekick or hostage negotiator.

## F_ _ _

Babies and children's immediate reaction to danger, preventing them sustaining injuries such as during a fall.

# Decision Making in Fear

Firstly, it's important to recognise that all of those reactions are not decided or thought through.

Secondly, any decisions that are made out of fear are made with the one aim to STAY ALIVE.

If your safety, or that of your children was not at risk, you may well think through and make informed choices with your decisions. We will come to decision making later in the course. But if you feel you cannot make decisions, it is likely because of fear or someone has told you you can't.

We'll work on that.

notes.....

# Guilt

Guilt definition - a feeling of responsibility or remorse for some offense, crime, wrong, etc., whether real or imagined. https://www.dictionary.com/browse/guilt

Let's take a look at guilt, there are things that we all feel guilty for. But let's put it into the context of the Bill of Rights and boundaries. Guilt feels awful, but it's meant to, it's designed so you realise that you have done something wrong. You learn from it, you apologise and you don't do it again.

Dealing with guilt.

Have a think about something you feel guilty for and run through the questions, is it guilt or a guilt trip? If it's guilt then apologise, or at least recognise that and learn from it.

Guilt Trips.

Definition - to make (someone) feel guilty, especially in order to induce them to do something. If it's a guilt trip, put it down. It's not yours to carry.. Not sure? Run it by a friend or professional.

# Guilt Checklist

Guilt & Guilt Trips

Did you overstep someone's Bill of Rights?

Did you overstep someone's boundary?

Were you aware that you were stepping over their boundary?

If your answers are yes to 2 or more, then you may have something to feel guilty about. Follow the guide below.

If the answers are no, then this is possibly a guilt trip.

## Guilt Action List

- Recognise what you have done.
- Apologise for what you did.
- Acknowledge how that made someone feel.
- Don't do it again.
- An apology is empty if you don't learn from it and change the behaviour.

# Guilt-Trip Checklist

## Guilt & Guilt Trips

Did you overstep someone's Bill of Rights?

Did you overstep someone's boundary?

Were you aware that you were stepping over their boundary?

If your answers are 'no' to 2 or more, then this is possibly a guilt trip.

Definition - make someone feel guilty, especially in order to induce them to do something.

If your sense of guilt comes from what you perceive as an inadequacy for never doing enough or being good enough, regard it as a guilt trip.

# Guilt Action List

Refer to the guilt check list. Complete the actions you need to complete if there is something you feel guilty for. Remember if you have recognised it as a guilt trip, then the step is to unburden yourself from it.

STEP 1

STEP 2

STEP 3

STEP 4

STEP 5

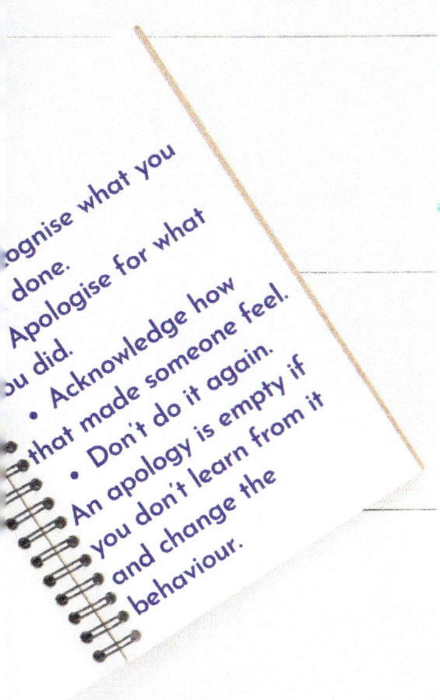

# Where Do You Feel The Feelings?

Use the body diagram and add each emotion one at a time, Grief, Fear & Guilt. Write the words, draw the shapes & colours, are they heavy? Light? Sharp? Soft?

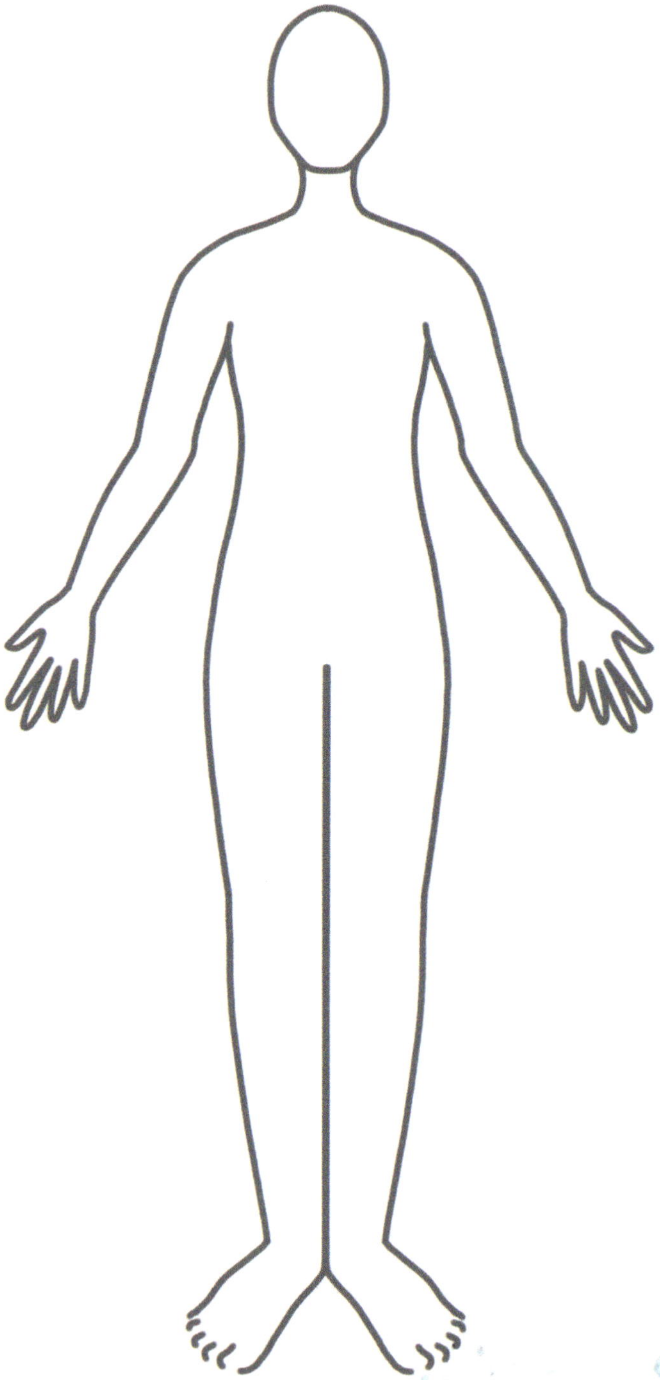

" BE ENOUGH FOR YOURSELF FIRST. THE REST OF THE WORLD CAN WAIT "

LIFE ON PURPOSE MOVEMENT

# Thoughts, Feelings & Actions

Each factor affects the other, creating a downward or upward spiral. When you change your actions, your thoughts and feelings change and vice versa.

Do something differently in your self-care routine this week and watch the spiral change. Small steps in the right direction can have a massive effect on your well-being.

# SELF-CARE - COLOURING

Colouring in or doodling really helps our minds process information.
We are making connections with our left and right brain, making it easier to process information.
Feel free to doodle or colour in whilst on our course. Or, set some time to do this as part of mindfulness.

More Positive Me CIC 2021

# CHECKLIST - 4

**Well done! Take your time to process all that you have learned in Chapter 4. Feelings are meant to be felt. There are no wrong & right feelings, they are there to tell us something. They dissipate when we face them.**

- [ ] I completed the 'Cycle of Grief' recognising that it isn't a straight line and there is no specific timing or route for the journey.
- [ ] I completed the 5 'F's, they are fight, flight, freeze, friend & flop.
- [ ] I completed the guilt & guilt trip check lists. (Revisit the Bill of Rights to help you recognise the difference. )
- [ ] I completed the guilt action list. (Use the notes at the bottom of the guilt trip check list to help you.)
- [ ] I have ecognised how thoughts, feelings and actions impact and influence each other. Become aware if the spiral down & the spiral up. and endeavour to change one thing.
- [ ] Self Care - I have had a go at colouring in or doodling. (You don;t have to be an artist, the joy is in the doing.)

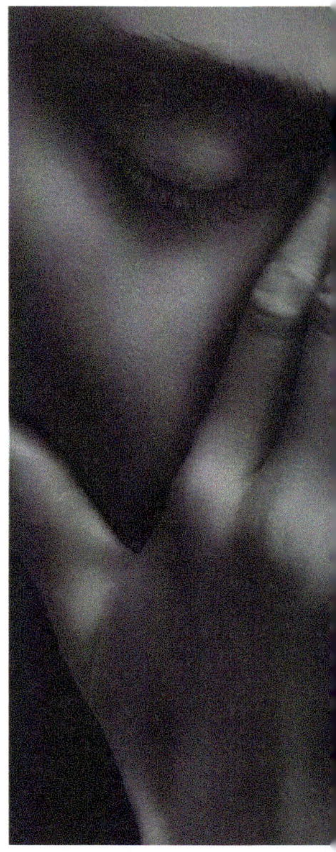

# Chapter 5

## Anger

# CHAPTER 5
# ANGER

We continue emotions with an exploration of anger, understanding its purpose and recognising the difference between anger and aggression.

- What Is Anger?
- Anger vs Aggression.
- How Does Anger Feel?
- Suppressed Anger.
- Healthy Ways To Release Anger.
- Clay Exercise.
- Self Care. - Hydrate.

## The main aims of this chapter:

- To explore anger as an emotion.
- To distinguish between anger and aggression.
- Look at how to deal with anger appropriately.

# What is Anger?

Let's explore what anger is. Write as many words as you can that relate to anger.

# Anger vs. Aggression

Did you use the word 'aggression' or 'violence' or something similar?

These words are not anger as an emotion, they are actions. Someone may use these actions when they are angry in order to assert control or dominance.

Anger is an emotion we feel when something is not right. When we don't know what to do with anger, it can spill out into aggression. We may also be scared of anger, in which case we lock it away and are physically unable to feel it.

"Anger is a normal feeling.
It's ok to feel angry but it is NOT ok to be aggressive with other people. You should always acknowledge feeling angry and find a healthy way to get that feeling out."

" In this chapter,
I recognised a clear distinction between aggression and anger. This was hugely important to me when going through the process of my recovery."

Anger, when harnessed correctly, is a game changer. It's an essential part of your healing journey, allowing you to set clear boundaries and say to yourself, "I am not accepting that behaviour." It does not need to be vented as aggression, it can be assertive, confident and healing. This means that you know your self-worth and your Bill of Rights and will not be taken advantage of.

# How Does Anger Feel?

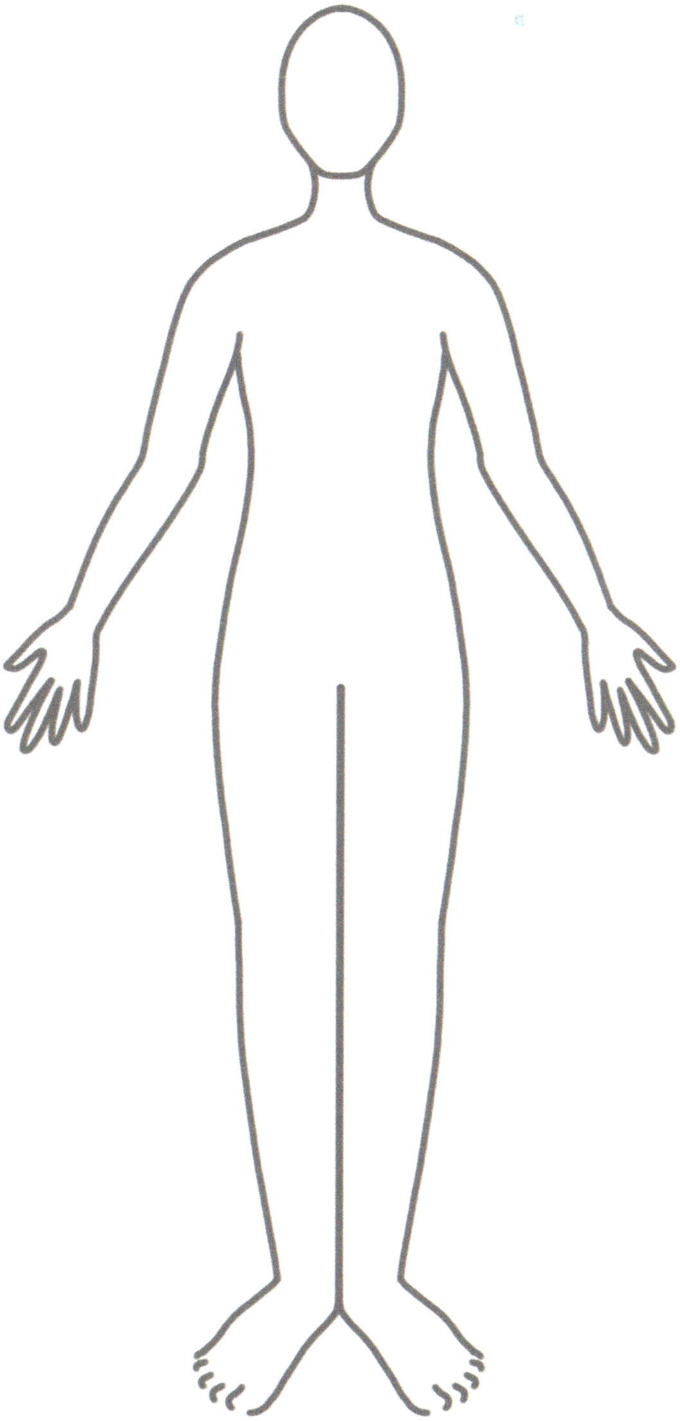

Use the body diagram and add words to show how anger feels for you. If it's not anger that you're feeling because you can't find it, use the words that explain how you *are* feeling. You can use colours and shapes to help show what's happening within your body when you can't quite feel it.

# Suppressed Anger

The problem is, when we avoid this anger, it can cause other issues. That energy has to go somewhere. It goes into our muscles and causes issues such as fibromyalgia, ME, exhaustion, etc. It can also affect your mental well-being and memory.
https://www.learning-mind.com/repressed-anger/

"I thought it was wrong to be angry or feel anger as it would put me in the same place as my abuser. I did not want to be anything like them and felt that getting angry would make me abusive myself."

"I was not able to feel angry and I felt very tense and on edge a lot of the time. I felt unable to relax and also found myself tearful and crying very often. After learning about anger and looking back, I do believe that some of the tears I was having were from anger and were not all from sadness as I had first thought. The added pressure I put on myself by not allowing myself to be angry or feel anger, was so unhealthy and I believe contributed towards my chronic pain."

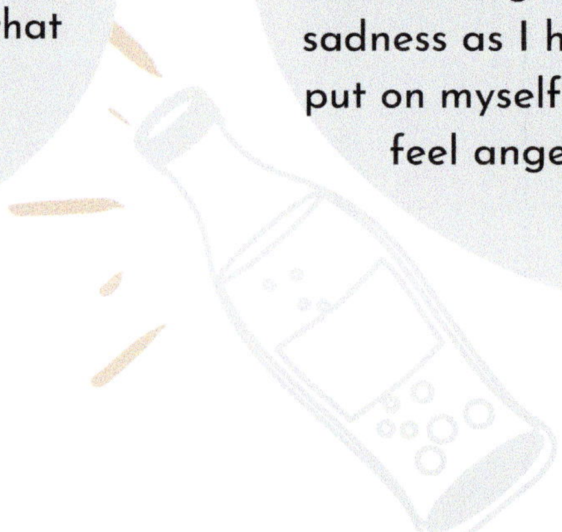

A great way to visualise anger 'exploding' is a fizzy drink bottle. When we shake it but release the lid slowly it dissipates. When we shake it, shake again, shake it some more and then release the lid, anger spills out everywhere. So instead, we should find healthy ways of releasing our anger so that it doesn't 'bottle up'.

Often, it is a straw that breaks the camel's back. Things build up and then it can be one small thing that makes you boil over. Aggression is about regaining control - it appears that someone has 'lost control' and so it's designed for regaining it back. If an abuser has gotten angry (aggressive) and smashed or broken things, did they break their own things or something of yours?

So something that appeared 'out of control' may have merely been to regain control. After all, they wouldn't do that in front of their boss, would they?

# Healthy Ways to Release Anger

Anger is an energy therefore, when we suppress anger, it makes us ill. Finding healthy ways to release anger is really important.

**Exercise i.e running**

**Take Up Kick Boxing or something similar**

**Bottle Bank**
A great safe way to smash glass and release that anger

**Play Loud Music & Dance Around**

"Let it out, don't bottle it up. I found writing an angry letter helped me. I could say what I liked within the letter without overstepping anyone else's boundaries and also keeping myself safe! You can either then rip up the letter and bin it or burn it."

"I have spent a lifetime surpressing my anger. I felt I had to be passive and discreet so that I would not be seen. However, I learned that I had every right t feel angry. Facing this anger and allowing myself to feel angry has made me feel much happier."

# Clay Exercise

Angry Clay

Happy Clay

- Take two balls of modelling clay and an open bin.
- With your first ball, mould it with your hands and think about all the things you are angry about, (or should be angry about).
- Start to say them out loud.
- Feel the emotions.
- When you are ready, throw the clay into a bin.
- Wash you hands.
- Now with the other clay, start to mould it and think of happy things, the things you are grateful for.
- Make something out of the clay.
- This can be whatever you want. Popular choices are hearts, caterpillars & stars, but make what you want.
- Leave it to dry.
- **It's important that you don't reuse the angry clay!!**

# Self Care - Hydrate

Yes, we get it, water is boring! Water is bland, it's flavourless or, if you drink tap water, you may find it has an odd taste that you don't like very much. The truth is, without water our bodies do not function.

When we dehydrate we feel unwell, head-achy, hungover and in the long term it can lead to health problems. If you are not used to drinking water, I doubt you even have a thirst for it. But, when you get into the habit of drinking water, you become thirsty and your body starts to crave it.

Did you know that when you drink water:

- Your kidneys function correctly, eliminating harmful toxins.
- You naturally lose weight.
- Your brain function increases.
- Your skin clears and brightens.... to name but a few benefits.

Imagine, if you will, a dry hanging basket. When you pour water in, it runs straight out. Now if that hanging basket is watered daily, it doesn't run out, the basket retains it. That's what we need for our bodies.

# CHECKLIST - 5

**You are doing so well! Anger is a really difficult one if you just can't find it inside as it can be quite scary when you have always associated it with aggression. Remember to separate the two.**

- [ ] I found as many words as possible that associate with anger.

- [ ] I now ecognise the distinct difference between anger, a healthy emotion, and aggression, an action to gain control.

- [ ] I have drawn and coloured in how anger feels to you withing your body and mind. Added words to describe the feelings and where they are felt.

- [ ] I have filled in the post-it notes on healthy ways to release anger.

- [ ] I completed the clay exercise or set a day & time to do so. Great one to do with the kids! Remember to chuck the angry clay away and was your hands before starting on the happy clay.

- [ ] I read all about hydration and have made a plan to drink more water. (You could add cups to your journaling pages and fill each one as you have one.)

# Chapter 6

## Boundaries

# CHAPTER 6
# BOUNDARIES

We look at values and beliefs and the importance of setting boundaries.

- Values & Beliefs.
- What Is A Boundary?
- Colouring In Exercise.
- Boundaries In Relation To Your Bill Of Rights.
- Consequence.
- Self-Care - Positive Self-Talk.

## The main aims of this chapter:

- To gain an understanding of boundaries and the feelings associated with setting them.
- Recognising healthy boundaries, with everyone - not just partners or ex-partners.
- Explore healthy ways to protect your boundary. and the importance of doing so.

# Values & Beliefs

We are all unique. Even identical twins will have different tastes in food, enjoy different hobbies etc. Let's look at what makes you, YOU! Take a look at your influences through childhood that we have already covered. Did any of them have an impact on what you do now? What are your values and beliefs?

# Values & Beliefs

My perpetrator's values and beliefs. Where are they the same as yours? Where do the clash?

# Notes

"The beliefs & values I was brought up with; respect, loyalty, politeness etc, were always there throughout my time with my abuser, but a lot of the times this was knocked down and not accepted by my abuser and I was sometimes even told that I was brought up wrong. I have always had my inner core beliefs and values and I wanted to stand up for myself, but I guess the fear factor took over and it was easier to accept those of my abuser, rather than keeping my own. I felt that the course helped me realise this, and definitely helped me in finding my inner 'ME' again."

Now take a look at your abuser's values and beliefs. Where they matched, you really connected. Where they don't match there will be a clash, not just a difference of opinion, but a proper full on clash. So you either went with their way of thinking, or you started to no longer have an opinion about it as it hasn't been validated. What's more, your abuser has probably heavily criticised someone else for having an opinion similar to yours, so you have kept quiet. This has more than likely been done intentionally. The things that you connected on, were what drew you in.

# What is a Boundary?

Put your bill of rights in the middle. Your boundary is to protect that, as are others' boundaries to protect their own. But what if you didn't even know you had this bill of rights? What if you've never tried to put in a boundary, or if you have someone that just trashes it anyway, so what's the point? The point is, you cannot function and be the most awesome version of yourself possible without that boundary. You cannot gain the respect of others (or yourself for that matter) without a boundary. Maybe you built a stone wall two meters thick and so high that even the best person could not reach you. You built it as protection, I know, but the best boundary is more like a picket fence. People know it's there but don't go over it. If they do, they soon learn the picket fence is there for a reason and they need to respect that. Now imagine there is no fence at all and all those people are trashing your lawn because they didn't know, care or realise that it was your space.

We know when our boundary has been overstepped as it makes us feel awful.

"A boundary is a personal rule, line or limit we set of things we allow or disallow others to cross. Depending how we feel about a situation."

"A boundary is my core beliefs and values of my own self & worth, basically honouring yourself as an individual with your own needs and wants. These boundaries are put in place to keep myself safe and make sure people respect my own core beliefs & values. They are also so we can see and respect others' boundaries as well. Whatever they may be"

## Colour in the centre circle with your favourite colour.

Now, think about people who have overstepped your boundaries. Give them an outer circle and a different colour. Describe what they did to overstep each boundary, add their colour on top of yours, in your circle.

Now your colour is muddied by those stepping all over your boundaries.

## Colour in the centre circle again with your favourite colour.

Now, with each person that overstepped, put a boundary in place . Write down how you would do this with each scenario on the previous page . Give them all the same colours as before.

Now your colour stays true and not muddied by those stepping over your boundaries.

"YOUR PERSONAL BOUNDARIES PROTECT THE INNER CORE OF YOUR IDENTITY AND YOUR RIGHT TO CHOICES"
GERARD MANLY HOPKKINS

# Boundaries & Your Bill of Rights

Let's take a look at the Bill of Rights again. A boundary can protect your Bill of Rights.

We can choose where our boundary is and when we feel the right to do that, we gain others' respect.

If someone oversteps our boundary, we need to let them know, otherwise the behaviour continues.

There needs to be consequences for disrespecting your boundary deliberately.

We also need to respect the boundaries of others and be a role model to others.

# Consequence

So what happens with those who are used to trashing our boundaries? How do we reinforce those boundaries?

Consequences look like:

- First time: 'Please do not do that again, I do not like it'
- If it happens again: 'I've asked you not to do that, please'
- If it happens again: ' I have now asked you twice, if it happens again (insert consequence)'

When you are learning to do this, it's quite easy to fall foul of setting an extreme consequence. For instance, with children: 'Right, that's it you are grounded for a month!' But the issue here is, are you going to be able to maintain that? Because, if not, your consequence will go right over their head because they are used to you setting a boundary but not seeing consequences through.

Ask yourself: 'Is the consequence reasonable?' And 'Does it seem fair?'.

notes

notes

You are going to have to practice and practice even more. If you set something reasonable and achievable, then you are more likely to succeed and have a much better result next time. For example, turning off the internet until the teenagers' rooms have been tidied after asking them to do it and warn that there will be that consequence. Then do put the internet back on once they do what has been asked.

# Positive Self-Talk

Negative self-talk, we all do it, we are our own biggest critics. Do you find when someone puts you down, that your inner critic joins in to reinforce those negative beliefs? It's so important that you learn to turn that around. It eats away at your self-esteem and it stops you from becoming everything you can be.

Negative talk sends us on a downward spiral, we want an upward spiral. Of course, this takes practice, and that's why we are here. Small steps in the right direction. We believe in you, when you start to believe in yourself, that's when the magic happens. You are enough.

Firstly,
start recognising when you do it.

Secondly,
be curious, ask yourself why you do this? Explore your ideas. You may want to start a journal and write your thoughts down. This really helps you to process information and make sense of it. Write down what it was you said to yourself, i.e 'I'm stupid', 'I can't', 'I'm not good enough', and then write down how you feel about this.

Thirdly,
think about how you could be nicer to yourself, after all you wouldn't talk to a friend like that, so become your own best friend.

"I'm always putting myself down and I find it very difficult & uncomfortable to receive compliments. My self-talk and self-worth is something I still have to really work on. I'm my own worst enemy, picking fault at myself wherever I can! "

" I WOULD RATHER ADJUST MY LIFE TP YOUR ABSENCE THAN ADJUST MY BOUNDARIES TO ACCOMODATE YOUR DISREPECT. "

# CHECKLIST

Complete the checklist before moving on to the next chapter.

- [ ] I explored and completed my values and beliefs.
- [ ] I chose my core colour.
- [ ] I have completed the task of people overstepping my boundaries.
- [ ] I have completed the task putting boundaries in place for the people that overstepped my boundaries.
- [ ] I made notes about setting consequences.
- [ ] I started to reframe my negative self-talk.
- [ ] I will now complete seven days of journal pages.

# Chapter 7

## Behaviour Types

# CHAPTER 7
# BEHAVIOUR TYPES

We explore the main different behaviour types and their characteristics.

- The Behaviour Types Line.
- Behaviour Types & Your Bill of Rights.
- Recognising Behaviours.
- Explore Passive.
- Explore Aggressive.
- Word Collection On Assertive.
- Explore Assertive.
- Explore Passive Aggressive.
- Self Care - Gratitude.

## The main aims of this chapter:

- To recognise different behaviour types.
- To learn about body language, traits and the link to our Bill of Rights and boundary setting.
- Practice gratitude.

"TO BE PASSIVE IS TO LET OTHERS DECIDE FOR YOU. TO BE AGGRESSIVE IS TO DECIDE FOR OTHERS. TO BE ASSERTIVE IS TO DECIDE FOR YOURSELF. AND TO TRUST THAT THERE IS ENOUGH, THAT YOU ARE ENOUGH." - EDITH EVA EGER

# The Behaviour Type Line

In the box below write the word PASSIVE at the left hand side of the line.

Passive is accepting or allowing what happens or what others do, without active response or resistance.

Write the word AGGRESSIVE on the right hand side of the line.

Aggressive is behaving or done in a determined and forceful way.

Write the word ASSERTIVE in the middle.

On the curve, write the words PASSIVE AGGRESSIVE.
Passive Aggressive can be the behaviour that either a passive person or aggressive person skips to, as they aren't aware, or don't feel comfortable with assertiveness. This can present as sarcasm, talking behind someone's back or using the excuse 'it was only a joke.'
Quite often, a passive person can jump to aggressive and then straight back into guilt ridden passive again.

# Behaviour Types & The Bill Of Rights

Let's look at that line of behaviour again. As a passive person becomes more assertive, the aggressive person will see that as a threat (moving towards them on the line). As you begin to be boundaried and protect your Bill of Rights, the aggressive person see's this very act as infringing on their rights! This attempt to be assertive with an aggressive person will raise your risk. We advise not trying this while in an abusive relationship and this is the very reason this book is for 'after' domestic abuse.

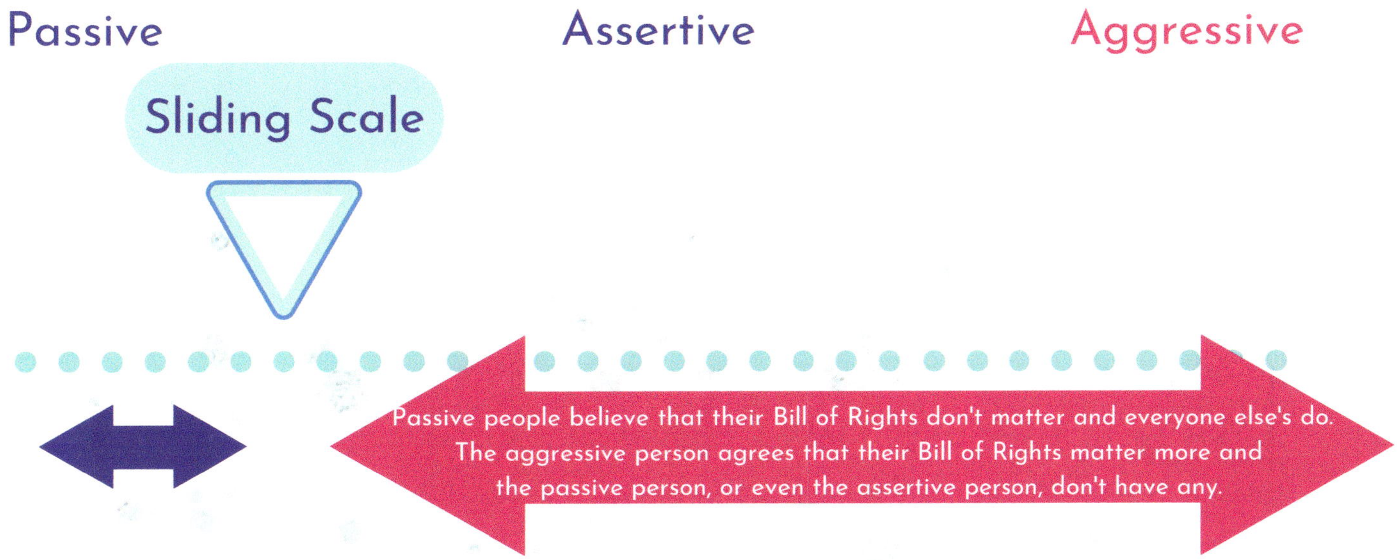


Two assertive people would be able to meet in the middle, respect their own and each other's boundaries and Bill of Rights.

"I do believe that assertive is the healthiest place to be so that you're respecting your own bill of rights as well as others."

# Recognising Behaviours

*Passive* has kept you safe when you have felt under threat. Not confronting anyone if you are not happy about something, not believing in your rights, believing that someone else's rights are more important than yours, or not being in a position to make choices for yourself. Passive behaviour looks like: lack of eye contact, head down, rounded shoulders, speaking quietly, saying sorry all the time etc.

*Aggressive* behaviour doesn't respect anyone else's Bill of Rights, only their own. It is dominant and intimidating behaviour with the sole intention of control. It's loud, big, direct eye contact, right up in your personal space, it is threatening and violent, either physically or psychologically.

*Assertive* says how they feel and suggests a solution. Confident, tall in posture, well dressed/shows that self-care is an essential part of their life. Has clear boundaries, firm but fair. Ensures their Bill of Rights is respected and respects others' Bill of Rights and boundaries in equality to theirs. Healthy communicator. Has a good work life balance.

*Passive Aggressive* always cracking jokes, will use sarcasm and 'jokes' to make digs but if challenged will deny it and accuse you of being too sensitive or dismiss it as 'banter'. It can look similar to aggressive or can even be mutters under the breath. Holds resentment and never quite gets the results they want but will continually moan about it. Does not respect boundaries, has little boundaries of their own or continually moves the goal posts.

# Passive Behaviour

## Behaviour

- You don't express your own wants, needs or ideas.
- You ignore your own rights.
- You allow others to take advantage of you.
- You don't say what or how you feel.

## Reason

- To avoid conflict or confrontation or possible injury.
- Because you don't know any other way to be.

## Result

- Anger
- Resentment
- Shame
- Frustration
- Powerlessness
- Feeling used, trapped, defeated, helpless & out of control.

## Example

### Behaviour

You avoid talking to your solicitor. You call your solicitor's secretary and say "Please ask the solicitor to call me." You complain about your solicitor's irresponsible behaviour to your family and friends. You constantly worry about the situation.

### Reason

a. You are concerned about offending your solicitor.
b. You are afraid that if you are direct your solicitor may get angry.
c. You don't know how to tell your solicitor that you are upset and why.
d. You believe that a solicitor is an important person + so it would be wrong to raise your concerns.

### Result

a. Your solicitor continues not to return your calls.
b. Your solicitor never knows that you are upset and why.
c. You continue to pay for a service that you are not receiving.
d. You continue to worry about your holiday plans.
e. You feel bad about yourself because you are unable to deal with a situation that upsets you.

# Passive Behaviour

Let's explore.....

## Body Language

i.e. lack of eye contact

## Actual Language

i.e. apologising all the time

## Beliefs

i.e. your needs are more important than mine

## In Conjunction with the Bill of Rights

i.e. The Bill of Rights don't apply to me

"I recognised it and knew I needed to become more assertive and not let people keep walking over me. This is harder to change than it looks, and I am still working on it."

# Aggressive Behaviour

## Behaviour

- You express your feelings and needs at the expense of others.
- You violate the rights of others.
- You try to dominate.

## Reason

- You are angry.
- You want to achieve your goal.
- You don't want to deal with other
- person's feelings.
- You don't know any other way to be.

## Result

- Still feeling guilty, angry and hungry for power and control.
- You are abusive to others and can be violent.
- You destroy relationships.

## Example

### Behaviour

You call your solicitor's secretary and scream at him or her because your "damn" solicitor hasn't returned any of your phone calls.

### Reason

a. You don't know any other effective way to express your anger and frustration.
b. You have tolerated your solicitor's irresponsible behaviour for so long that you have just "had it."
c. In your family, when people are upset, they yell and scream.

### Result

a. Your solicitor labels you as "crazy & hysterical" and feels justified in not returning your calls.
b. You feel embarrassed and guilty as you "lost it" on the phone.
c. You have no resolution.
d. You feel bad and powerless because you haven't changed the upsetting situation

# Aggressive Behaviour

Let's explore.....

Body Language

Actual Language

Beliefs

In Conjunction with the Bill of Rights

# Assertive

How many words can you find that describe assertiveness?
Who do you know that is assertive?

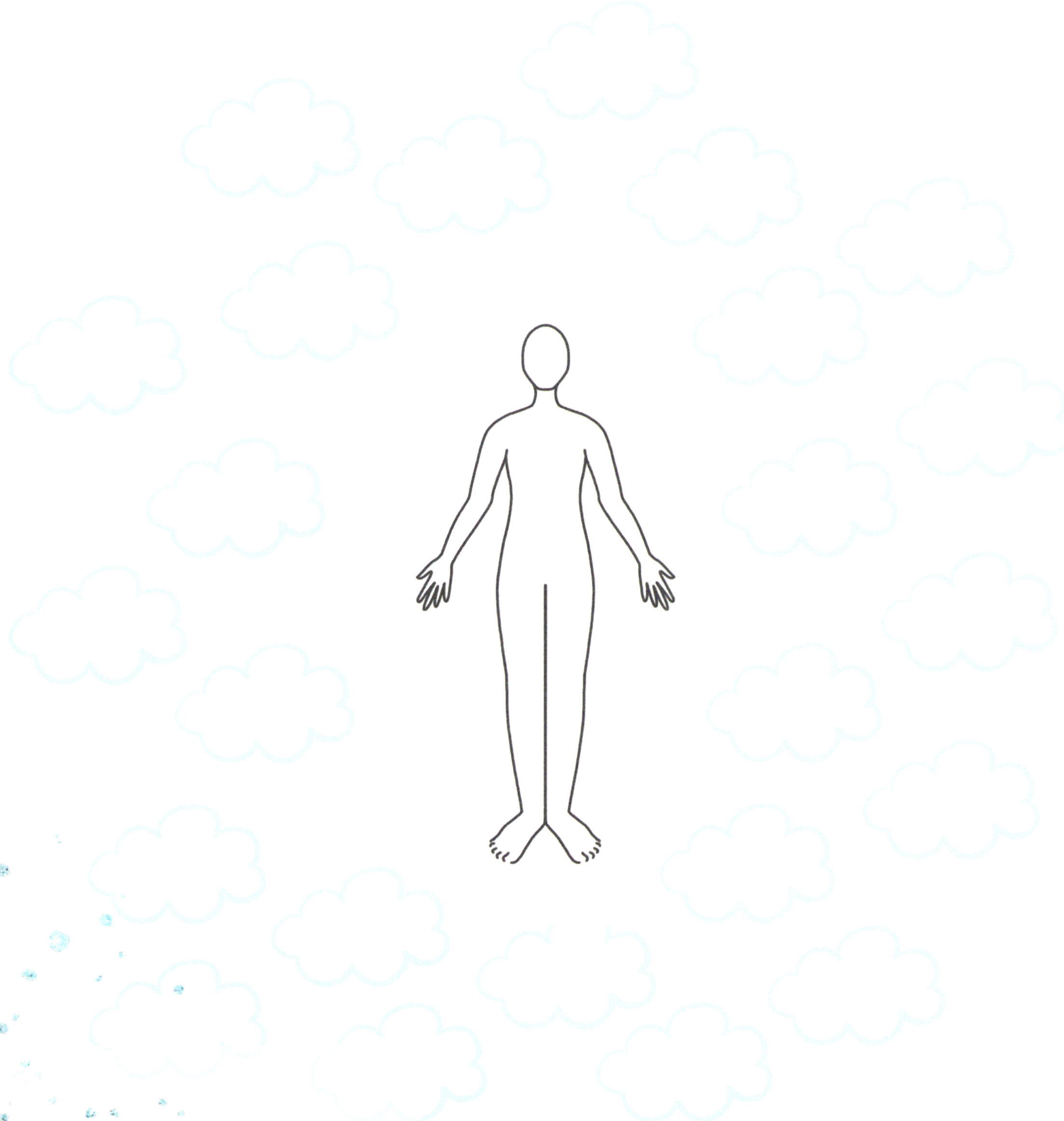

# How does it feel when you are unable to be assertive?

Feel defeated, helpless, inadequate & out of control

Unable to set boundaries or be assertive

Often used or abuse by others

"I was fearful of becoming assertive, standing up for my rights and upsetting others around me as I have been passive for so long and had so many people control me. I found it very difficult to change things. It's not just my abusive relationship I was getting controlled in, but also a lot of other factors in my life. I almost felt trapped, that I could not live the life I wanted for myself for fear of upsetting others."

# Assertive Behaviour

## Behaviour

- You express your own needs or feelings without violating the rights of others.
- You are honest, sincere and direct.

## Reason

- To set boundaries
- To gain direction
- To achieve your goal to treat yourself as an equal, valuable person.
- To show you are worthwhile.
- To create honest, healthy relationships
- To become empowered.

## Result

- You gain respect.
- You feel proud, powerful, worthwhile, sincere, self-directed and in control of your own life.

## Example

### Behaviour

You call their office and speak with the secretary – "I'm upset because my phone calls haven't been returned. I need to make certain that my court date is not scheduled for when I'm on holiday. I expect a call from him (or her) by 5pm today."

### Reason

a. You want to be clear with your solicitor that you are upset that they haven't returned your calls.

b. You want to be able to plan your holiday without worrying about the court date.

c. You want to give a time by which you need to be contacted – giving some structure to the solicitor.

### Result

a. Your solicitor knows that you are upset.

b. Your solicitor knows why you are upset.

c. Your solicitor knows what behaviour you now expect.

d. You feel better about yourself because you have taken steps to gain some control of an upsetting situation and have set some boundaries with an irresponsible solicitor.

# Assertive Behaviour

Let's explore.....

Body Language

Actual Language

Beliefs

In Conjunction with the Bill of Rights

# Passive Aggressive Behaviour

Let's explore.....

Body Language

Actual Language

Beliefs

In Conjunction with the Bill of Rights

" YOU ARE NOT LAZY, UNMOTIVATED OR STUCK. AFTER YEARS OF LIVING YOUR LIFE IN SURVIVAL MODE, YOU ARE EXHAUSTED. THERE IS A DIFFERENCE. "

NAKEIA HOMER

# Gratitude

Have a think this week of the things that you are grateful for. Start the process of focusing on the 'haves' rather than the 'have nots.' Not only is it good for your mental health, but it will improve your self-esteem. Assertive people practice gratitude. Write three things you are grateful for every day on your journal pages. Here are some suggestions:

| | | |
|---|---|---|
| Sunshine | | Friends |
| Somewhere to live | | Internet |
| Pets | Nature | |

# CHECKLIST

You're doing so well! Take a moment to check that you have covered everything in this chapter before completing your 7 days of journaling.

- [ ] I have completed the Behaviour Line with Passive on the left, Aggressive on the right, Assertive in the middle and Passive Aggressive on the curve
- [ ] I have recognised the 4 different Behaviour Types.
- [ ] I have found as many words as I can that I associate with Assertive and added some people that I regard as assertive.
- [ ] I have completed Passive.
- [ ] I have completed Aggressive.
- [ ] I have completed Assertive.
- [ ] I have completed Passive Aggressive.
- [ ] I recognise the behaviours in conjunction with The Bill of Rights and my Boundaries.
- [ ] I will complete the 7 Days journaling and the gratitude practice before starting the next chapter.

# Chapter 8

## Assertiveness

# CHAPTER 8
# ASSERTIVENESS

We explore assertiveness and learn some techniques including how to have an assertive conversation.

- Your Guide To Being Assertive.
- 3 Assertiveness Techniques.
- Making A Request.
- Why Is It Hard To Make A Request?
- Why Is It Hard To Refuse A Request?
- Self-Care - Mindfulness.

## The main aims of this chapter:

- Discover the 'I' message and put it into practice to protect your boundaries and Bill of Rights.
- To practice making and refusing requests.
- To identify the 3 assertive techniques.

"HEALING DOESNT MEAN THE DAMAGE NEVER EXISTED. IT MEANS THE DAMAGE NO LONGER CONTROLS OUR LIVES."

RAWFORBEAUTY.COM

# YOUR GUIDE TO BEING ASSERTIVE

1. Determine exactly what your goals are, exactly what do you want to accomplish or change?
2. Choose your wording carefully, use an 'I' statement where appropriate and be brief.
3. Practise your statement, alone, in the mirror or with a friend.
4. Address the situation as soon as possible. The longer you postpone setting a boundary, the harder the situation will be to change.
5. Prepare yourself that other people may not like the fact that you are setting a boundary with them. If the exchange gets out of hand, end it.
6. Avoid using the word 'you' - as in "I'm angry because you ignore my feelings." Stick with "I" and talk about your own feelings and expectations - as in "I'm angry when my feelings are ignored". 'You' suggests blame and puts the other person on the defensive.
7. Avoid pointing your finger at the other person, it is an aggressive gesture and may put the other person on the defensive.
8. Avoid raising your voice, an assertive voice is slightly louder than normal conversation.
9. Avoid giving an ultimatum. Ultimatums are aggressive and usually result in escalation of a problem situation.
10. If you are seated at the time of the encounter, sit slightly forward in your chair - this posture suggests confidence.
11. Keep constant eye contact without staring or glaring, this shows confidence, poise and purpose.
12. Have your facial expression agree with your message. If you are serious, look serious. Try not to smile or laugh if you are delivering serious news, no matter how nervous you may be.
13. Stop yourself if you feel a need to apologise for being assertive or raising a point. An apology implies that it is somehow improper to be setting a boundary, which is never the case.
14. Repeat your statement if necessary.

# 3 Assertive Techniques

We will look at;

- "I" messages
- Broken record
- Escaping from an out-of-control encounter

They allow you to...

- Successfully choose wording for your statements.
- Ensure that your words are heard & taken seriously.
- Exit gracefully from a difficult situation.

# THE 'I' MESSAGE

The 'I' Message takes practice. We are making it clear that we are not putting the blame on anyone, just expressing our feelings, needs and wishes around a situation and suggesting a solution. You are ensuring your boundary is clear. You have no control over the other person's response or reaction, but you do have control over how you respond and react.

The Scenario. You have been waiting for days to hear back from your solicitor about the court hearing date as you have a holiday booked and don't want it to clash and you be unavailable.

STEP 1

__Identify your feelings__

e.g. "I'm upset because..."

STEP 2

__Describe the situation in a non-blameful way.__

e.g. my phone calls haven't been returned.

STEP 3

__Explain the effect of the behaviour on you.__

e.g. I need to make certain that my court date is not scheduled for when I'm on holiday.

STEP 4

__Describe what behaviour you would like to see instead.__

e.g. I expect a call from him (or her) by 5pm today."

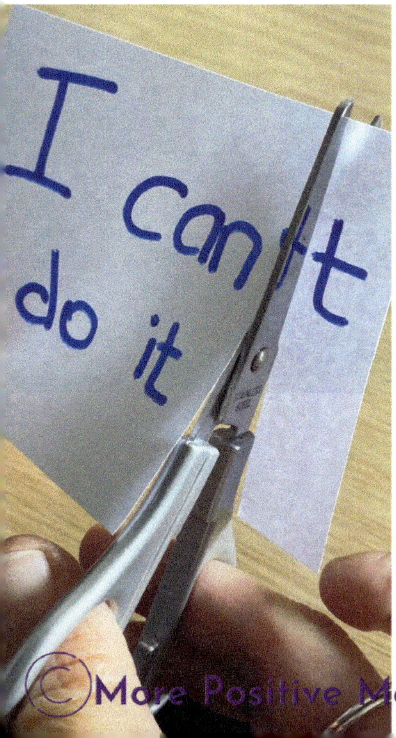

# THE 'I' MESSAGE

Have a go yourself

STEP 1

I feel...

STEP 2

When...

STEP 3

I feel...

STEP 4

I would prefer if...

# BROKEN RECORD & ESCAPING FROM AN OUT OF CONTROL SITUATION

## Broken Record

Imagine a salesperson calling, they have used their charm and technique to keep you on the phone. 'I'm not interested' has gone over their head. Broken Record is literally repeating what you have already said. If they are not getting it, you can end with 'I have already told you (enter how many times) and you are not listening to me therefore I am ending the call, goodbye' and put the phone down. You could just put the phone down, but its good practice and they are used to it, they love unboundaried people!

## Escaping An Out Of Control Situation

There is a third way of reinforcing a boundary, its known as 'Grey Rock' or Stone Walling'. Unfortunately there will always be people who don't respect our boundaries, these are usually people taking advantage of us. If no other way of reinforcing a boundary works, then using this technique and refusing to engage in any conversation can sometimes be necessary.

This includes situations when the other person begins to get nasty, ridicules you, becomes sarcastic, insults you, makes an aggressive gesture, or begins a verbal barrage.

Remember your safety comes first and an abusive person will see assertiveness as a threat.

# Making A Request

Example: Sam, I need to ask you a favour. Could you possibly babysit my two children this afternoon from 1 until 3? I just got a call that my doctor's appointment has been rescheduled and I don't want to miss it."

My Request...

How did it feel to make that request?

Is this the kind of request you would feel comfortable making?

Why/why not?

Why is it difficult to make a request?

# Why Is It Hard To Make A Request?

Fear of rejection.

We might think that making a request means using someone.

Remember that you have the right to make any request. You assume responsibility for accepting the other person's answer.

A need to be in control.

Lack of self-worth.

## Suggestions For Making Requests

Do not begin by apologising for the request that you are about to make.

Do not beat around the bush - get right to the point.

Be specific, give as much information as possible so that an informed decision can be made.

# Refusing A Request

Example; Sam, I need to ask you a favour. Could you possibly babysit my two children this afternoon from 1 until 3? I just got a call that my doctor's appointment has been rescheduled and I don't want to miss it"

Your response to refusing this request ...

How did it feel to refuse the request?

Is this the kind of request you would feel comfortable refusing?

Why/ why not?

Why is it difficult to refuse a request?

# Why Is It Hard To Refuse A Request?

It seems selfish.

Not knowing how to say 'no' assertively. Remember that you have the right to refuse any request.

We want to be liked by everyone. A person who respects your rights will like you even if you say no.

We want to appear to handle everything.

It might be dangerous. Safety must be the first priority.

<u>Suggestions for refusing a request</u>

When you say 'no', say it clearly and without any detailed explanation.

Remember, you can postpone your decision.

If you refuse a request, you can choose to invite the person to ask you again - but only if you really mean it.

Minimise your apologies.

# SELF-CARE MINDFULNESS

Do you find yourself dwelling on the past or worrying about the future?
Is your head overwhelmed with a list of things you must do? Do you have panic attacks when it all gets too much, or maybe you get to a point where you keep making mistakes? Maybe your mind buzzes with overuse, like an old computer struggling to keep up, or is that just mine? Imagine your mind constantly contracted like a muscle. Mindfulness helps us relax that muscle, giving our minds a break and a chance to heal. It's all about the present, coming back to where you are, grounding.
We lead such busy, hectic lives. Here is how to give mindfulness a go. Use your senses, ask yourself the questions:

What can I see? What else ..?
What can I hear? What else ..?
What can I feel? What else ..?
What can I smell? What else ..?
What can I taste? What else ..?

If you really stop and take note, you become aware of so many different things. Mindfulness can be used in everything we do. The more you practice, we suggest five times a day, the more peace you will find. There is happiness in the wonder around us, just being in the moment. Really notice the here and now, give yourself a break from the hurt of the past and the anxiety of the future.
For panic attacks, use the above technique but count down from five. Five things I can see, four things I can hear, and so on.

# CHECKLIST - 8

How was the assertive session for you? It gets easier with practice. Knowing and believing in you Bill of Rights and your right to protect them with a boundary is key here. Remember to journal to process this.

- [ ] I have read through and taken note of the 15 suggestions for being assertive.

- [ ] I identified the three assertive techniques and look at them in relevance to your situations.

- [ ] I have nderstood the broken record technique and endeavoured to practice when the next salesperson calls.

- [ ] I recognised the importance of your safety first when a discussion becomes out of control.

- [ ] I will ttempt some mindfulness and added it to my self care routine, journaling about what comes up for me with this weeks session.

# Chapter 9

## Red Flags

# CHAPTER 9
# RED FLAGS

We look at the warning signs, Red Flags, that a relationship may be abusive. We look at the green flags too.

- Recognising Red Flags.
- Relationship Journey Scanario.
- Problems, Conflicts and Disagreements.
- Green Flags.
- How We Are Impacted.
- Self Care - Digital Detox.

## The main aims of this chapter:

- To recognise early signs of abuse.
- To understand fair ways of communicating.
- To recognise healthy relationships.

# Recognising Red Flags

- Is your partner excessively jealous or possessive?
- Are they charming one minute and then abusive the next?
- Do they have sudden changes of mood – like Dr. Jekyll and Mr. Hyde?
- Are they stopping you from seeing your family and friends?
- Do you feel isolated?
- Are they constantly criticizing you and putting you down in public?
- Do they embarrass you, often in front of family and friends, so that you are seen in a bad light?
- Does your partner play mind games and make you unsure of your own judgment?
- Do they tell you that you're useless and couldn't cope without them?
- Do they control your money?
- Do they tell you what to wear, who to see, where to go, what to think?
- Do they pressure you to have sex when you don't want to?
- Are you starting to walk on eggshells to avoid making them angry?
- Do they monitor your movements? Or check up on you via your email, Facebook, Twitter or by looking at your text messages?
- Do they use anger and intimidation to frighten you and make you comply with their demands?
- Has your partner ever threatened you, or intimidated you by using violent language or smashing up the furniture?
- Are you forced to alter your behaviour because you are frightened of your partner's reaction?
- Are you blamed for their behaviour e.g. they say you were "asking for it" or that you deserved the abuse?

Adapted from Womens Aid

# Red Flags

We call warning signs 'Red Flags', something that happens that we can recognise as a warning sign to an unhealthy relationship.

In this scenario, we look at a heterosexual relationship with a female target of abuse. This, however can play out in any kind of intimate relationship, so please adapt to suit your needs. The scenario follows a relationship from the very beginning. Read it thoroughly and then add some red flags next to the things that you think may be a warning sign. This scenario can be repeated with a green flag, looking out for the healthy relationship signs. A red flag does not mean this relationship is abusive, but it is a warning sign. It helps you recognise the areas where you might have to think and have a conversation. It would then be from the conversation and received response, that you would know if it was becoming abusive or not.

Notes

# The Relationship Journey Scenario

Sandy met Danny online through a dating app. She was visiting friends in York and decided she would see if there was anyone worth meeting up with while she was in town. Sandy had a young child and had recently gone through a divorce so she was not looking for any kind of commitment.

She got chatting to a guy who seemed sweet and would text her during the day to see how she was and what she was up to. They spoke on the phone and text quite a bit. Sandy felt as though she knew him before they had even met. Sandy went to stay with her friends and suggested to Danny that he get some friends together so they could all go out for the evening as she didn't want to abandon the friend she was visiting. Danny said none of his friends were available, so he came alone.

The evening went well, but Sandy wasn't sure. There was something not quite right, but she couldn't put her finger on it. She was flattered that he paid her so much attention and appeared to be besotted with her.

The next day, she met Danny for lunch after chatting to her friends who said they really liked him and thought Sandy could do with the attention after going through such a horrible time with her ex-partner. Danny seemed more at ease and he made Sandy laugh which she hadn't done for a long time. Sandy ended up going back to Danny's place and they spent the afternoon in bed. The sex was great.

When Sandy returned home, the texts and calls continued. He asked if he could come and visit the following weekend. He did, bringing flowers. He stayed the weekend and Sandy's son appeared to enjoy his company. Very quickly, their relationship grew. Sandy would drive 200 miles on the weekend to visit Danny and Danny would do the same once a month.

After 12 weeks of dating, Danny asked Sandy to move in with him. It didn't take her long to say yes. After all, she would be around the corner from her friends too. Within 6 months Sandy had sold her house and moved the 200 miles to be with Danny.

Even before she unloaded the van, Danny smacked her son's legs as he was swinging them and it got on his nerves. This shocked Sandy, but nothing was said and her son behaved around him. Her son started a new school. The money she got from the divorce paid for the renovations on Danny's house. Danny insisted that Sandy didn't have to work, but that she could take a little job at her son's school so that she was home for him in the holidays and after school. Danny became quite strict with Sandy's son and told her she spoiled him.

Do you recognise any Red Flags?

Put the Red Flags on the scenario in the places they appear.

# More Red Flags

| | | | | |
|---|---|---|---|---|
| Cheats on you | Alcohol or drug abuse | Playful use of forced sex | Blames others | Possessive |
| Unreliability | Acts differently around others | Invading your privacy | Cruel to animals or children | Verbal mistreatment of others |
| Imposing their opinion | Charmer | Jealousy | Dislikes your family and friends | Moving way too fast |
| It's all about them | constant texts & 'love bombing' | Lying | Secretive | Belittling your opinion |

"I was fairly lucky as one thing I have had is a strong reliable family. I have had parent's that have respected each other's boundaries and even when they have over stepped the mark, they know how to react as adults and have been married for 46yrs. I wanted the Disney fairy tale ending, I wanted the happily ever after, and I tried very hard to get that, and no matter how hard I changed and did what the abuser wanted, it still wasn't good enough, everything was my fault. I realised, and not until after doing this course, I was never going ever get my fairy tale ending in that relationship at all! No matter what I did! "

"He would always find something to get aggressive abou or to control me with. My relationship was so unhealthy anc full of Red Flags, and without thi course, I would never of seen or known any of this!"

# Which Red Flags do you recognise now, that you didn't before?

# Problems, Conflicts and Disagreements

**Healthy**

Both win by growing understanding in the relationship

1. No fear of violence or verbal abuse.
2. The current issue and disagreements are discussed.
3. Honest communication of feelings, using assertiveness techniques.
4. Speaking one at a time.
5. Agreed on 'Time Out' when tensions rise.
6. Respect for one another.
7. Willingness to say "I'm sorry " and mean it.

**Unhealthy**

The person in control wins over the other

1. The threat of abuse is always present.
2. The current issue gets clouded, by bringing up past problems etc.
3. Denial of facts and attempts to put partner on the defensive.
4. Constant interruptions, ignoring and/or refusing to talk.
5. Tensions escalate to the point of explosion.
6. Personal insults and name calling.
7. Refusal to admit when they are wrong and tendency to blame others.

Just because there is a red flag, does not mean a relationship is or will be abusive. View them as warning signs, have an assertive discussion. When we address the issues we can then tell buy their reaction or response that the relationship is abusive or heading that way. Remember safety first.

# Green Flags

## Qualities that healthy relationships share

**Commitment**

Promoting each other's welfare and happiness. They value the unity of the family.

**Coping Ability**

Members of healthy relationships view stress or crises as an opportunity to grow.

**Appreciation**

People in healthy relationships show appreciation for one another.

**Spiritual Wellness**

Healthy relationships have a sense of greater good or power in life and that belief gives them strength and purpose.

**Communication**

Healthy relationships have good communication skills and spend time talking with one another.

**Time**

People in healthy relationships spend quality time with each other.

# How We Are Impacted

## In relation to our core and boundaries

In relation to our core and boundaries, in healthy relationships we can see our healthy core colour. When we are together, we merge to create an 'us' colour as we work as a team, but allow each other to still be who we are. In an unhealthy relationship, you can see the abusers colour overshadows, ours so we can't shine.

Unhealthy

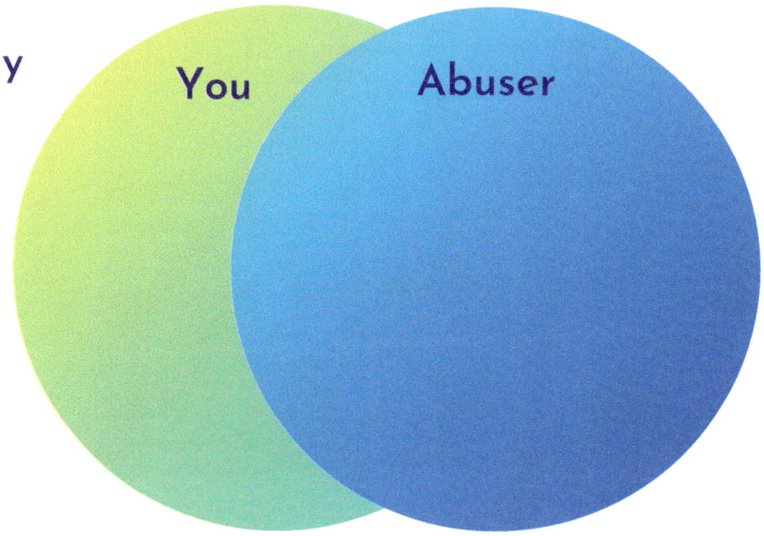


Healthy

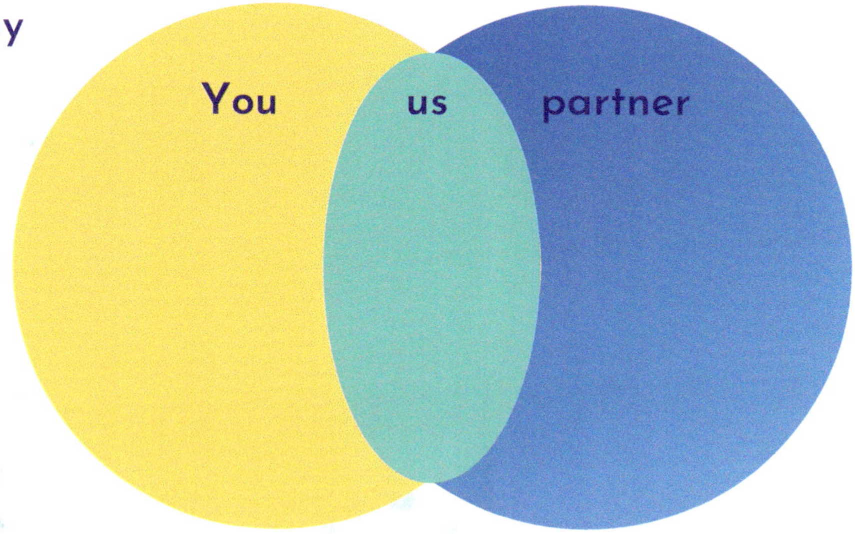

# SELF-CARE - DIGITAL DETOX

It's not that long ago that we didn't have all this technology. Where it is fantastic at connection, it's very apparent that it can consume our lives. On average we check our mobile phones every 7 minutes. Look at ways to digital detox this week.

Endeavor to put your phone down when in company.
Choose a time to check your social media or take a break from it.

My plan

Schedule a time to use the computer and don't spend more than 2 hours, 30 minutes in front of a screen.

My plan

Make your bedroom tech free, or endeavour to turn off the screens at least 30 minutes before you want to sleep.

My plan

# CHECKLIST

Congratulations! This week, hopefully, is a chance to reflect and move forward in new relationships with your new found boundary and assertiveness skills. Your past does not need to impact on future relationships.

- [ ] I have recognised Red Flags as warning signs.
- [ ] I added Red Flags to the relationship Journey Scenario.
- [ ] I recognised the different Red Flags and added your new ones to your flags.
- [ ] I recongised the difference between fair & unfair problem solving to conflict, & disagreements.
- [ ] I understand Green Flags, signs that a relationship is healthy and added Green Flags of my own.
- [ ] I completed some ideas around digital detox and endeavour to address this or just become 'aware' through this week.
- [ ] I will now complete my journal over the next 7 days and reflect on this week's learning.

# Chapter 10

## Decision Making

# CHAPTER 10
# DECISION MAKING

We explore decision making and our belief that we can't make decisions or that when we do, it's always the wrong decision.

- Great Decision Makers.
- How To Make a Decision.
- My Decision.
- Pros & Cons / For & Against
- Self-Care - Declutter.

## The main aims of this chapter:

- To understand decision making in a new light.
- To work through steps for making decisions.
- To start to lose the fear that can surround decision making.

# Great Decision Makers

We can almost guarantee if you are reading this book, or taking the course, you have decided you are not a good decision maker. Not because you are bad at making decisions, but because you feel or you have been told or led to believe that you are no good at making decisions.
Quite frankly, you are a good decision maker, you just don't know it yet.
When we make a bad decision, we only find out it's a bad one after we made it, after it's gone wrong. We also have a habit of looking for the evidence to reinforce that. 'Remember that time I made a bad decision? Now that's going to affect every decision I make because I'm just not good at it'
.Here's the thing, hindsight is a wonderful thing. If we knew how a decision was going to pan out before we made it, it would be a whole lot easier.

You make decisions all the time. You decided to read this book, do the course. You decided what to wear today, what to eat. Even if you decide not to make a decision because either it's too hard, or you decide to leave it until someone else decides for you or leave it to chance or fate, this is still a decision you have made.

It can be quite surprising that when you start running the options by other people, you really already know what you want - you just don't know how to go about it.

# How To Make a Decision

1. Define the problem and set a goal.

What is it that you are struggling with and what are your options? There may be more than a couple of options available.

2. Ask for expert advice.

This could be a professional, a friend, someone with experience or whom you trust etc.

3. List alternatives.

Remembering to step away from black & white thinking. Are there any other alternatives to consider?

4. Look at the consequences of each.

Do any options have a negative impact and what are these?

5. Weigh the pros and cons of each.

You may find the pros and cons (also known as for & against) very imbalanced, thus helping you with the decision.

6. Make a decision based on reason, not emotion, balancing your negativity and unrealistic romanticism with objectivity.

The best decisions are made in balance with the heart & head.

# My Decision

1. Define the problem and set your goal.

2. Ask for expert advice.

3. List alternatives.

4. Look at the consequences of each.

5. Weigh the pros and cons of each.

6. Make a decision based on reason, not emotion, balancing your negativity and unrealistic romanticism with objectivity.

| Pros | Cons |
| --- | --- |
| | |

Looking at the pros & cons can really help you look at the imbalance that usually occurs around decision making. Writing it down helps you focus, especially when it's running or spinning through your head.

" IF THE VERION OF YOU FROM FIVE YEARS AGO COULD SEE YOU RIGHT NOW, THEY'D BE SO PROUD OF YOU. KEEP GOING. "

TINYBUDDA.COM

# Self-Care - De-Clutter

Have you ever heard the phrase cluttered head, cluttered home? Or is it the other way around?

There is a clear correlation though. Just organising and having a clear-out of even a drawer can have a positive impact on you. Be careful of being overwhelmed though. You may have a whole house to do and then resort to de-cluttering nothing. You could work through your wardrobe, under the bed, a kitchen cupboard, or a bathroom cabinet. Is there something you are keeping a hold of that really doesn't belong in your life anymore? If you are de-cluttering your mind, write it down and decide how to let it go. It could be a paper airplane into the bin, scrunched up and thrown onto a fire. Be creative and make de-cluttering a little project this week. If you don't have time today, schedule a time to do it. Note how you feel after achieving this and congratulate yourself. Create a de-clutter schedule. You could create three piles as you start to have a clear out. One pile to throw away, one for the charity shop and one to sell on ebay or at a car boot sale.

# Setting Intentions

Set intentions to de-clutter & set a goal

1 - How often are you going to de-clutter?

2 - What will you start with?

3 - I will complete .... by ....

4 - Or I will work for (amount of time)

5 - By the end of the week I will....

# CHECKLIST -10

A shorter chapter, but very impactful and life changing. Take time to journal your thoughts around decision making and keep practicing.

- [ ] I have read the page - great decision makers
- [ ] I have processed the information on how to make a decision.
- [ ] I have given the decision making process a go.
- [ ] Did you make a decision? Journal about it on your pages.
- [ ] I have decided where to start with de-cluttering this week. Even the smallest of steps in the right direction is progress.
- [ ] I will journal my thoughts and feelings through the week to help me process my new skills.

# Chapter 11

## Goal Setting

# CHAPTER 11
# GOAL SETTING

We explore goal setting, how to create realistic goals and look at effective ways to achieve them.

- Obstacles to goal setting
- Cycle of Change
- SMART goals
- 6 month plan
- 5 year plan
- Vision Board
- Self-Care Get Moving

## IN THIS CHAPTER YOU WILL LEARN:

- The importance of setting goals to help you move forward.
- How to set SMART goals.
- How creating a vision or dream board can make a substantial difference to your future.

# Goal Setting Obstacles

When you started this course, you set yourself a goal. The mere fact that you are up to this section now, means you're doing pretty well at achieving this goal! So what did that take? What did you need to do to make that happen? We doubt, with everything you have been through, that it just 'happened.' Write down your obstacles and how you overcame them.

# Cycle of Change

Learning new behaviours takes time, determination and practice.
Each relapse is not a failure if we learn from it and start again.

# SMART Goals

We use the acronym SMART for goal setting to make them more achievable. Here's how.

SPECIFIC - be specific about what your goal is and what it is you would like to achieve. Think of who, what, where and when.

MEASURED - track your progress and measure outcomes.

ACHIEVABLE - make sure the goal is reasonable to achieve.

RELEVANT - is the goal worthwhile and does it meet your needs?

TIMELY - set a time in which to achieve the goal to keep you on track.

# My SMART Goal

MY GOAL IS -

SPECIFIC -

MEASURED -

ACHIEVABLE -

RELEVANT -

TIMELY -

# Climbing The Mountain

Do you know that the wealthiest and most successful 1% of people in the world all have something in common. They set goals and they review them constantly until they achieve them. Then they go ahead and set some more.

So how do we do this? It can be pretty daunting to look at the top of a mountain and not even try to get up there because it feels impossible.
We break it down into steps. Each step is possible on its own, each one moves you a little closer to your goal.

So now we have a goal and its SMART. But how do we get to the top of the mountain? We add some steps. Put your goal at the top, and you on the bottom step. Now work out the steps you need to do to get to the top. Each step may not be equal, but they all play an important role to get you there. Just like this course, it has been broken down into steps.

Look at you, almost at the top!

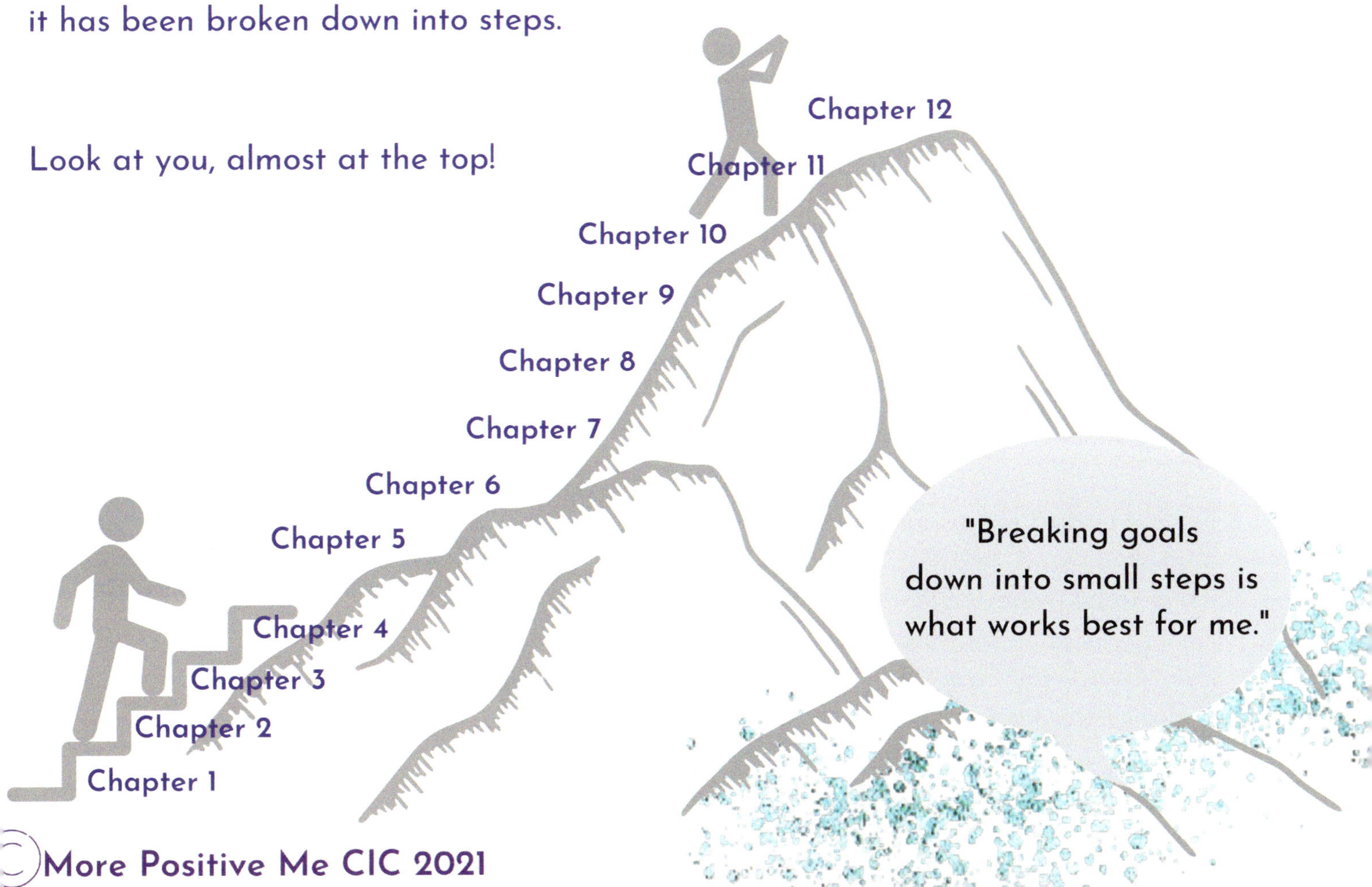

# 6 Months From Now

Have a think about where you want to be in 6 months time in the different areas of your life.

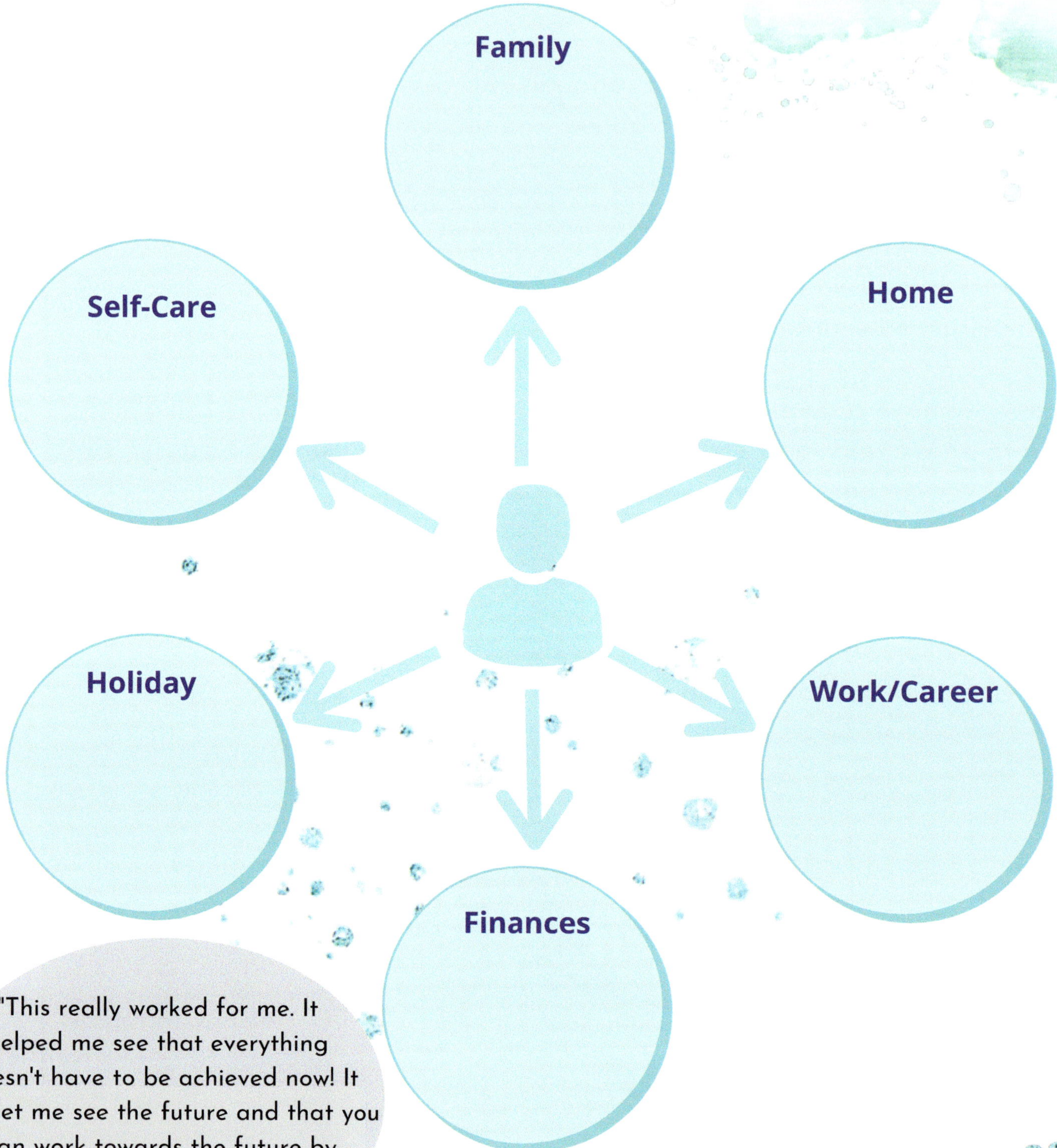


"This really worked for me. It helped me see that everything doesn't have to be achieved now! It also let me see the future and that you can work towards the future by breaking it down in order to get there."

# 5 Years From Now

Have a think about where you want to be in 5 years time in different areas of your life and think even bigger!

**Family**

**Self-Care**

**Home**

**Holiday**

**Work/Career**

**Finances**

"My finances were a mess
but I set a goal of owning my own
ome in 5 years. I had no idea how I
ould do it, but within 5 years I had
y own house. I think just setting the
goal gave me focus, rather than
just drifting."

# Vision Board

## Also known as mood or dream boards

Having something in front of us keeps us reminded of our goals and the things we would like in our lives.

Collect images from magazines that you are drawn to. They don't have to make sense but you do need to feel a connection to them. Trust your instincts.

Use a piece of cardboard or an old picture frame and stick your collection on with a glue stick.

Put your piece of art up somewhere where it will inspire you on a daily basis.

"I found this therapeutic and a reminder when I look at it, of things I like and things that I want to achieve."

What have you discovered by doing the vision board?

# Self-Care - Get Moving

This weeks self-care is about getting moving. However much you exercise, let's look at increasing it. It is shown that 30 minutes to 1.5 hours of exercise, 2-3 times a week, not only improves our physical health, but our mental health too. What works for you? The gym isn't for everybody, just as country walks aren't for others. Find what works for you, be curious, explore, give different things a go. I tried yoga and found it hilarious, then gave pilates a go and discovered that it's just right for me.
You can count your steps with a pedometer, or free app on your phone and then set step challenges with friends. Have a go at something new this week, or at least book it in your diary for a future date.

"MAY THE SEEDS THAT YOU PLANT TODAY, BE THE FLOWERS THAT BLOOM TOMORROW"

MRS. EASTON

# CHECKLIST

Tick off the checklist once you have covered everything in the chapter. You are nearly there, well done.

- ☐ I have recognised my goal setting obstacles.
- ☐ I have looked at the cycle of change in relation to my own experiences.
- ☐ I have read about SMART goals and set myself a SMART goal to work to.
- ☐ I have created a vision board, or started to collect pictures to create a vision board.
- ☐ I have decided where I want to be in 6 months time in all of the areas of my life.
- ☐ I have decided where I want to be 5 years from now and added them to the page. (It is important not to skip this.)
- ☐ I have decided on a plan of self-care to get moving and either set it as a SMART goal or looked at it in conjunction with the cycle of change.
- ☐ I will complete 7 days of journaling and reflect on this chapter before I go to the final chapter. (Write your thoughts and feelings to process what you have learned.)

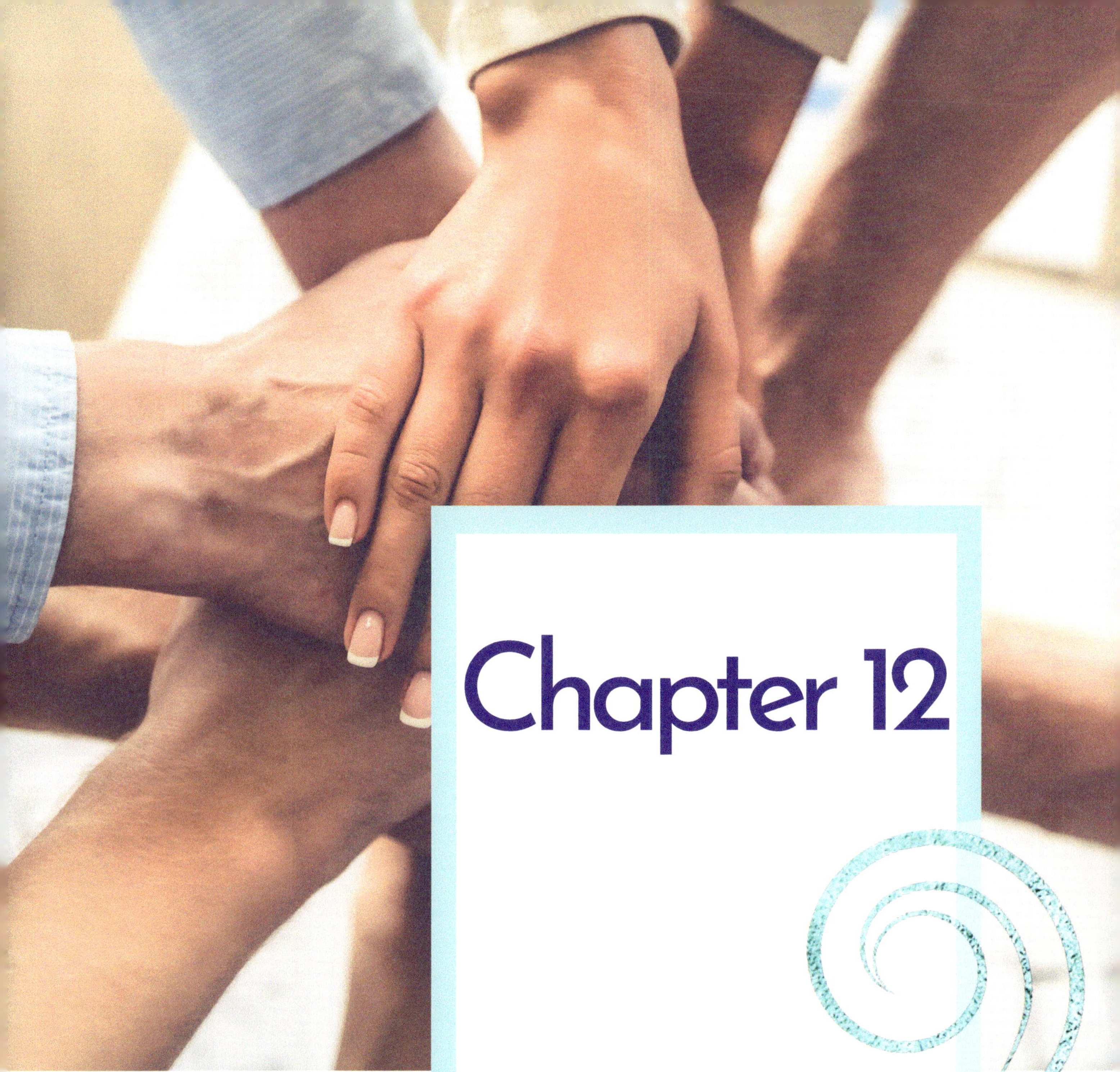

# Chapter 12

## Endings and Beginnings

# CHAPTER 12 ENDINGS AND BEGINNINGS

We look at how far you have come through your journey of empowerment and look at what's next for you.

- Revisit the chapters
- Revisit mountain people
- Revisit course expectations
- A letter to myself
- What's next for you?

Look at the journey travelled since starting this book/course.

Celebrate how far you have come.

Look at what's next for you. It's not the end, it's just the beginning.

# CHAPTER RECAP

Let's look through the Chapters to see how far you have come. Write some notes if you want to. Chapters 1, 2 & 3:

**Chapter 1 - What is abuse** - Your Bill of Rights - The Government Definition of Domestic Abuse - What is Domestic Abuse? - The Power and Control Wheel - The Cycle of Abuse.

**Chapter 2** - Why is it so hard to leave? - Family Roles - Excuses I Made - You are not responsible for the abuse.

Chapter 3 - Childhood Legacy - Influences through childhood - Family Roles - All or Nothing functioning - Healthy family traits - Unhealthy family traits.

# CHAPTER RECAP

Let's look through the Chapters to see how far you have come.
Write some notes if you want to. Chapters 4, 5 & 6:

**Chapter 4** - Cycle of Grief - Edwardian Window - The Science of Fear - 5 F's - Decision Making in fear - What is Guilt? - Guilt Trips - Dealing with guilt.

**Chapter 5** - What Is Anger? - Anger vs Aggression - How Does Anger Feel? Suppressed Anger - Healthy Ways To Release Anger - Clay Exercise.

**Chapter 6** - Boundaries - Values & Beliefs - What is a boundary? - Boundaries and your Bill of Rights - Consequence.

# CHAPTER RECAP

Let's look through the Chapters to see how far you have come. Write some notes if you want to. Chapters 7, 8 & 9:

**Chapter 7** - Behaviour Types - The Behaviour Type Line - Recognising Behaviours - Passive - Aggressive - Assertive - Passive Aggressive.

**Chapter 8** - Your guide to being assertive - 'I' message - Broken record - Escaping an out of control situation - Making a Request.

**Chapter 9** - Red Flags - Relationship Journey - Recognising Red Flags - Problems, Conflicts and Disagreements - Green Flags.

# CHAPTER RECAP

Let's look through the Chapters to see how far you have come. Write some notes if you want to. Chapter 10 & 11:

Chapter 10 - Great Decision Makers - How To Make a Decision - My Decision - Pros & Cons

Chapter 11 - Obstacles to goal setting - Cycle of Change - SMART goals - 6 month plan - 5 year plan - Vision Board.

My favourite part was...

Colour in the figure that most feels like where you are now and pop the date on the sheet. Now flick back to the beginning of the book and see if there is a difference in how you feel right now.

# Reflections

Reflect on the last 12 Chapters. What were your 'light bulb moments' where something suddenly made sense?

# Reflections

What were the parts you struggled with and will need more practice with?

# Letting Go

What do you need to let go of? What doesn't bring you joy? A physical 'letting go process' is really helpful. Try one of these:

Write everything on a list, scrunch it up and throw it into a bin.

Write everything on a list, then safely (outside) set fire to it or throw it onto an open fire if you have one.

Write everything onto a balloon and then pop it!

Write everything onto a piece of paper, fold it into a boat shape and let it sail down a river.

Be creative and think of your own way to let go.

# Setting Intentions

Take a look at your goal when you first set your intentions. Did you achieve it? If you didn't, now you know how to set goals. Add it to your intentions now and create a SMART goal.

Specific

Measured

Achievable

Realsitic

Timely

# A Letter To Myself

Write a letter to yourself, congratulating yourself on getting this far and cheerleading yourself on for a fabulous life ahead. Set a note on your calendar or in your diary to revisit this in 6 weeks time.

Dear

With all my love,

As we draw to a close of our book and course, celebrate your achievements. It's always here to recap, you could pay it forward if you find someone who you think would benefit. Every new pattern of behaviour needs practice, like learning to ride a bike. Keep persevering, but once you have it, life will improve. Maybe you have already seen some changes in your life.

# What's next for you? With endings, come new beginnings

What is next for you? Now you are great at setting goals, keep setting them, keep revisiting them, keep aiming higher and speak to yourself gently when things don't go well.

Over the next few pages are a list of books and courses we recommend, including our own. Self-Care is the one thing you can really get to grips with, this will improve your self- esteem & self-worth.

Control the controllable, the things that are within your control, and not the things that aren't. Practice the art of responding rather than reacting and remember you have the choice of where your energy goes. Just because someone throws the ball, does not mean you have to throw it back or even catch it.

# CHECKLIST

Your last checklist. Make sure you tick them all off before going on to your last week of journaling. Go you!!

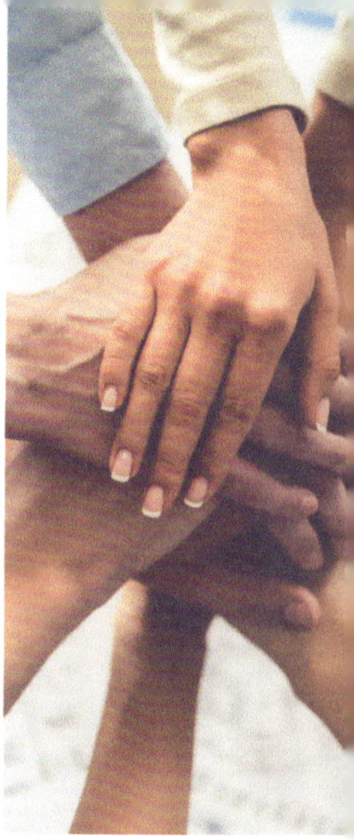

- [ ] I have taken the time to revisit each chapter and made notes.
- [ ] I completed the mountain people and then compared it to the one I completed in Chapter One. I made notes about the difference between the two.
- [ ] I revisited course expectations and made a note if this was achieved or not. I made a plan and set a goal to achieve this if I am not quite there yet.

- [ ] I wrote a letter to myself and made a note to read it again in 6 weeks.
- [ ] I decided what is next for me and set goals to revisit and made plans.

- [ ] I made a promise to speak kindly myself.
- [ ] I will endeavour to provide a testimonial or to share the course details or website with someone whom this course may benefit.

# INDEX

# INDEX

# Our Sources of Information

### Marylin Shear Goodman & Beth Creager Fallon

Pattern Changing For Abused Women. Written in (1995) to change the pattern of women returning to abusive relationships.

### The Government Definition Of Domestic Abuse

Current 2021, whilst the new Domestic Abuse Bill is being reviewed. www.gov.uk

### Power & Control Wheel

Adapted to be gender neutral from the Duluth Wheel. https://www.theduluthmodel.org/wheels

### Cycle of Abuse

Step by Step Guide to Understanding the Cycle of Violence - www.domesticviolence.org/cycle-of-violence

### Thought Feelings & Actions

Cognitive behavioural therapy (CBT)

### Suppressed Anger

www.learning-mind.com/repressed-anger/

### Recognising Red Flags

Adapted from Am I in an abusive relationship? - Womens Aid www.womensaid.org.uk/information-support/what-is-domestic-abuse/

video

# Our Sources of Information

### Great Decision Makers

Leonie Dawson - Shining Life + Biz - Leonie Dawson | Goals, Marketing + Creativity For Glorious Humans. Leonie has been a total legend with her courses for creating ecourses & writing books.
www.leoniedawson.com

### The Cycle of Change

Transtheoretical Theory of Change

### Cycle of Grief

A theory developed by psychiatrist Elisabeth Kübler-Ross suggests that we go through five distinct stages of grief after the loss of a loved one.

### Self-Care

Rediscovering You - A Self Care Toolkit. Created in partnership with Splitz Devon Domestic Abuse Support Service.

### Book Design

Done For You Divas www.doneforyoudivas.com & Canva canva.com

Funded by National Lottery Community Fund

COMMUNITY FUND

" SURROUND YOURSELF WITH THE DREAMERS AND THE DOERS, THE BELIEVERS AND THINKERS, BUT MOST OF ALL, SURROUND YURSELF WITH THOSE WHO SEE GREATNESS WITHIN YOU, EVEN WHEN YOU DONT SEE IT YOURSELF. "

# Books To Read

Lundy Bancroft

Why Does He Do That?
Inside the Minds of Angry and Controlling Men

The Joyous Recovery

Marilyn L. Shear Goodman and Beth C. Fallon

Pattern Changing for Abused Women: An Educational Program (Interpersonal Violence: The Practice Series)

Evan Stark

Coercive Control

Dr Jane Monkton Smith

In Control: Dangerous Relationships and How They End in Murder

Sue Penna

The Recovery Toolkit: A 12 week plan to support your journey from Domestic Abuse

Leonie Dawson

My Shining Year Life Goals Workbook

Marisa Peer

I Am Enough: Mark Your Mirror And Change Your Life

Johanna Hunter

Get Selfish- The Way Is Through

THANK YOU FOR PURCHASING OUR BOOK & ELEARNING COURSE. AS A COMMUNITY INTEREST COMPANY, EVERYTHING WE EARN FROM THE SALE IS PUT BACK INTO SUPPORTING PEOPLE IMPACTED BY DOMESTIC ABUSE.

Visit morepositiveme.co.uk/resources to see the most up to date resources, downloads, recommendations. and visit morepositiveme.thinkific.com to see our eLearning courses

Book & Course enquiries info@morepositiveme.co.uk

Professionals seeking licence to use this book with their service users please get in touch.

We offer licence and training to domestic abuse services and any professionals involved with victims or survivors of domestic abuse.

If you are a survivor and you have found this book has helped, please share with the professionals involved.

morepositiveme.co.uk
morepositiveme.thinkific.com
facebook.com/morepositiveme
twitter.com/morepositiveme
#empowermentafterdomesticabuse
#rediscoveringyou